SARA'S JOURNEY

A California girl through and through. Born in Los Ángeles, Sarita has lived within a 100 mile radius of LA all of her life. This is her story, that of a woman's journey of self-discovery, acceptance and forgiveness and is illustrated by the challenges that confronted her at the tender age of ten when her father murdered her mother, stripping Sarita and her five-year-old twin siblings of their mother's nurturing and love and leaving them in the care of her mother's family; her determination to give her young twin siblings the love they were cheated out of and the disappointments that ensued – laced with the deeply engrained religious beliefs and her Mexican culture that molded her into the woman she has become as told in this memoir of that metamorphic time in her life.

EVEN
when it's BAD *it's*
GOOD

SARITA PAREDES

ISBN: 978-0-692-15748-0

Hi, my name is Sara but most people call me Sarita.

Yes, I have a story to tell. You see, everyone always said, "Oh Sarita, you are so tough, how did you endure all that you've been through? You should write a book." Then I sat down to write my story and realized that even when it's bad, it's good. I was only ten when my father took my mother's life, leaving me and my five-year-old twin siblings without her love and nurturing. As a child, I was never fully aware of the truth behind her death, other than my father had murdered her. I only knew the different versions of the story that my mother's family and counselors had assumed. My father also had a different version of the story, but no one in my family ever saw the actual police report. Despite the difficulties, being tough was the only way I could survive. Now, as I sit to write, I realize that toughness became part of the fabric of which I am made.

DEDICATION

Because they are mine. Joaquin, Sarayi, Jordan and their children. God loves me so much he chose me to be your mother. I'm not sure how that worked out for you guys, but I think it's phenomenal! I get to say you are my children and that is my biggest honor. Life is filled with good times and bad times. Every day may not be a good day and that's okay. Good or bad there is always a lesson. Find it, learn it, and move on. Trust in God and trust in yourself. Don't dwell, don't settle and do not let anybody punk you, ever! Do more of what makes you happy and do it often. Forever and after – I LOVE YOU.

Because you chose me. Mercedes and Rafael Vasquez, you instilled in me Christian values, perseverance and honor. No other man in the world can fill his shoes. His great heart and humility are unparalleled, he lead by example, my Tio Rafael. She may frown upon some of my opinions and decisions, but she always has my back and keeps me in her thoughts and prayers. There's only one Merce like my Tia Merce. I thank God for blessing me with the both of you. My tio, you are gone now, and I will never forget you. If I was a dad, I'd hope to God I'd be at least half the dad that you didn't have to be. Thank you for loving me.

Because I am hers. She is the missing piece to my completely happy life puzzle, my mother. I am grateful for the time I got with you, and I am confident I will see you again. I still feel your love, thank you.

TABLE OF CONTENTS

CHAPTER 1

QUEEN OF ANGELS

*A*round me, the plane was packed with vacationers heading into Mexico, all talking, laughing and creating memories. All but us, our aunt Rosa, my brother and me. And, yes, of course, Dad. He was with us. Letting my eyes fall back to the carry-on I kept next to my feet, I became acutely aware of how long it had taken me to make this journey. Today, again, it seemed I was just doing what had to be done. Most people don't have two masses, but this seemed to be what was needed at the time. For me, sadness had sifted through my body like grains of sand, some getting stuck, while others went on through. Although we hadn't spoken in many years, I always knew my dad *was* there, that all I had to do was pick up the phone, but I never did.

I was looking out the window as we broke through the white puffy clouds, my eyes settled on the sheer expanse of the Sonoran Desert below me. Hermosillo sat in stark relief of the desert's vastness as far as my eyes could see, filling me with a strange sense of familiarity. I tried to sort through this uneasiness, then realizing for the first time, this feeling was that of emptiness, and it was a mere reflection of the emptiness below me now. That same emptiness I was left with after the grief and sadness I felt when my dad took my mom's life, shattering our small family, destroying our childhood, and then again, the day he died. Looking back down into the emptiness, my only consolation was knowing that the desert in all of what appears to be emptiness, isn't really empty at all. It is teeming with life. Hopefully, that abundance of life will find its way to me and rise in me as well. I am praying for my life to open to joy and possibilities, but a part of me knows I have to come to grips with my past in order to embrace the future.

About three months ago, my cousin, Paulette, and I had arranged for the first mass for my dad to be in English so his friends in the San Diego area who had gathered could feel more a part of it all. I found it all so strange. There was just something about the people, all strangers to me, who were gathering and who had been a part of his life. I felt a tinge of jealousy, maybe more than a tinge until I overheard the bits of conversation, and it made me realize the man they were celebrating was definitely not the man I knew when I was a child. Everything seemed so shallow. It didn't take long to understand that even they hadn't experienced his sweetness that I had known and loved many years ago.

I remember sitting in the pew, watching the people as they filed out of the church. Maybe twenty had come. I didn't count. I just remember how so many had come from all directions for my mother's funeral. She had been so loved. It was hard not to think of the journey I had been on that brought me to the church that day. It was a journey of coming to terms with my dad's past and his actions, trying to understand the man he had become and the man he once was. I was beginning to recognize this long path of personal growth that I had been on, and I still had so far to go. Although grateful for the progress so far, there were some things I had not forgiven nor processed. Ah, life is a journey, God help us!

I felt so uneasy, just sitting here as the plane soared through the sky. I wanted to walk, just walk, as my mind would not rest. This man I had loved so dearly, how had he changed so? As a child, I watched as he seemed more distant each day. By the time the twins were born, things were already changing. This man who was my guiding light seemed to have slowly faded until the man I adored no longer existed. It all culminated in the spring of 1987 when he killed our mother. But, on that day in San Diego, I came to realize we were here celebrating someone different. A different version of this man we called Father. And those who came to celebrate him were here for that other man, the man we never knew. Coming to this realization helped me to distance myself from it all and it left me wondering why in the world we did this. Why didn't we just take him home to be with his family in Mexico who loved all versions of him and let them celebrate the man they had loved? I realize now that distance is what I needed to get through it all that day, but now that distance was closing in. What mattered were the memories I had of my dad and the love that I still held for him, despite every-thing that had happened. I loved him to the ends of the earth and back, but how can we love someone who did something so awful to us, and can that deed ever be forgiven? Maybe it is a good thing we are coming into Mexico today, maybe here is where I will find my answers. Maybe my heart will open here in Guaymas, here, where his heart was rooted.

Time is so crazy, and we humans grab it and twist it around to make it work for each of us. For sure, time changes more than the hands on the clock. Maybe it is nothing more than as those hands slowly move around the face of the clock, we, as humans, allow that time to mark our change. Some of us grow and expand into better humans, while others of us rebel against growth and hover in our stagnant selves, while others still celebrate their dark side. I wondered where I fell into this.

I also realized that, just like time, our memories are ever-evolving and can shape the way we view our past experiences. I was grateful to have a few people in my life, like my dad's sisters, who could share their own memories of my dad and help me to see him in a different light.

.⧫⧫⧫.

We three kids had been treated as "other" for so long, always on the edge of the family. Everyone all expecting us to fail. I was determined to rise above them all – to show them, and then I ran out of "fucks" to give and I didn't really give a damn about what they all thought. Actually, I think I had spent too much time caring about what others thought. And the church and our Mexican culture played a huge role in all of this. It all fed into the depths of our pain, our shattered lives. I didn't want my mother's death to be in vain. Over and over, I told myself, I had to be resilient and rise above. I guess I was being a little petty also because I had to "show them" – the them being the "family". I was expected to be a loser and I was determined to disappoint them.

As I looked out the window at the clouds drifting by, that day in San Diego still sitting on my heart as if it was yesterday, that day I stayed silent, knowing I wanted to tell everyone to leave, that they didn't know this man. I needed time with my father. I so wanted to talk to him, even though he was gone. I needed to tell him why I never called. I didn't want to hear his lies, I just wanted desperately for him to understand I still had a deep love, something so deep and hidden that even I couldn't explain. I just needed him. I knew I couldn't put the pieces of this shattered life back together again, even though so many nights I would fall asleep dreaming of our lives back when we were whole, but I would feel the shattering, the moment he killed our mom, and I would wake in a panic. There is no going back. I took a deep breath. My silence that day was so unlike me where everyone could usually tell exactly what I was thinking, if it wasn't showing on my face, I was definitely voicing my opinion for all to hear. All of this left me wondering if I had hidden some of my deepest thoughts and feelings even from myself?

I realize now, I was the one who didn't know this man, the man I knew was gone long ago. I was still searching for the man I called Dad, searching, searching.... But gone. I wondered if bringing him back to Mexico would open us to a deeper understanding of our father.

Now, just trudging forward, just doing what was right. Inside that carry-on I had dad's ashes. When checking in, I didn't claim them. I had wrapped the urn in a towel and held on to the carry-on to be sure it was not lost in all the chaos of boarding. I knew I was supposed to acknowledge that I had the ashes, but it was no big deal, really. After all, if they discovered them, it wasn't like I was sneaking a body into Mexico. They would probably just charge me and ask me to fill out the paperwork I had avoided.

I looked down at the urn in my carry-on and felt a mixture of sadness and peace. I was finally taking my father home, to be with his family and to rest in peace. I didn't know what the future would hold, but I hoped that by bringing him back to Mexico, I could find some closure and maybe, just maybe, start to heal from all the hurt and pain of the past.

When we boarded the plane, I couldn't help but think about all the memories, good and bad, that my father and I had shared. The thought of him finally being at peace brought tears to my eyes, but at the same time, I felt a sense of liberation. I was ready to leave the past behind and move forward, to create new memories and find joy in life again.

I took a deep breath and closed my eyes, imagining my father finally being at peace and surrounded by love. And in that moment, I felt a weight lifted off my shoulders, a weight that had been there for far too long. I was ready to start my journey to healing, and I was ready to embrace the future, whatever it may hold.

My dad's sister, Rosa, was sitting next to me, and my brother was sitting across the aisle. As I glanced over at him, his face lacked expression, but that wasn't unusual, I hadn't been able to understand him these last few years. He had been a real jerk at the airport, acting like a spoiled teenager, moody as all hell, and I had no compassion for it all. It was like he wanted to tell me something, but he couldn't find the privacy we needed to do it. Now as I looked over at him, his face showed nothing. Everything was so different than how it all began. I pulled the carry-on up onto my lap, then leaned back and closed my eyes. The stress of it all was overwhelming and had been for weeks, months, years. The stress had my shoulders in a knot. "Be the good little soldier, Sarita. Just keep moving forward." Reminding myself that some thoughts were better left unsaid. I had told myself this for so many years, it wasn't surprising that it was here again.

"*Sarita! Quien nacio ahi?* Who was born there?" *My parents* would say as they drove past the Queen of Angels Hospital in Los Angeles.

"*Yo,*" I happily responded, all of three or four years old, and sitting on my mom's lap, back in the day before car seats were mandatory for children.

"Y quien is la reina de Los Angeles?" Who is the queen of Los Angeles, they would ask?

And I would respond. *"Yo,"* feeling confident and happy. They had me convinced that I was *La Reina de Los Ángeles* because I was born at Queen of Angels hospital. I truly believed and felt 100% *La Reina de Los Ángeles.*

Looking back now, this may be one of the reasons I felt I could do anything because they had truly made me believe I was different. I was a queen. Whereas the twins were never lifted up like this, at least not on a daily and constant basis. I don't know but think this could be part of it. The other part was because I was five years older than them, and they still needed our mother so much. One might say, I still needed my mother as well, but I had already stayed with Tía Merce, one of Mom's older sisters, for a time when the twins were born, so I had ventured out some.

How did my life turn from such simple sweetness to such pain and chaos? I felt as if my heart had been ripped from me. I shook my head and opened my eyes, knowing it was not the time for those thoughts, not now. My God! Where are these thoughts coming from, I wondered. I have never experienced these thoughts. It seems they had been blocked out completely. Could it be that I never ever questioned why all of this happened to me, to us? Was I so busy just keeping myself above water, that I never allowed myself to feel? To actually "feel"? The thoughts had broken loose now and were rushing at me from all sides, demanding attention. I don't want to think about this stuff. Just leave me alone, I begged the thoughts to stop. I was glad no one could see the rush of torment that seemed to be breaking loose within me.

I glanced over at my aunt. She had her eyes closed, which was good. Will it ever be time for me, I wondered, or will I always be on the outside, doing for others, caring about their feelings? Family, the Catholic Church, and our Mexican culture. The combination of the three could literally sink me, I thought. The realization made me shutter. I needed to get out and walk, to feel free. I wished we would hurry up and get there. I squeezed my eyes closed, rubbed them and then opened them again. The cabin of the plane seemed tight and more crowded.

I felt the softness of Rosa's hand as it slipped over mine, "It's almost time to land. Are you okay?"

"I'm fine. I'm just glad we're doing this, how about you?"

I didn't say, I'm glad I'm getting this over with so maybe I can get on with my life, but that was how I felt, or at least that was how I wanted to feel or how I thought I had a right to feel. God my heart hurts. Just thinking about all of this. Could I have been so callous? I sound like a selfish bitch, at least that's how I think I sound.

"Yes, it's time for sure, but coming home and knowing we are bringing your father back to his home...I'm so proud of you for doing this. Just so proud."

Bringing my father home. Now, in the quiet of the plane, I let myself embrace that idea. He is or was my father. But who surfaced in later years, I have no answer for, but thinking back at the Mass in San Diego, I was convinced this man that we had celebrated wasn't my father, but now I realized he actually was, but the dad I knew was buried deep into his soul. I wondered how these other layers smothered out the sweet soul we knew. What had happened to cause such a change?

I thought back to Tía Rosa saying, "I'm so proud of you..." It all depends on which aunt I'm talking to, and I have many, as to whether they are proud or not. I remembered the old saying, "Together we stand, divided we fall". That held true as well in our large Mexican Catholic extended family, but I was determined I would rise in the midst of them all. My aunts, my mom's sisters, helped to make our family whole while our mom was alive, while my dad's family kept their distance, even my dad refused to be anywhere near Mom's family. After her death, it was her sisters who reinforced their edges to protect the three of us kids. At least that was how it felt until things again started to change.

Family means everything, and the house full of happy, laughing relatives would warm my heart on any given day, as well it should, but that wasn't what we had. Family never did encircle us with love. We were all separate in our celebrations, but being devout Catholics, the sanctity of family was right up there next to Godliness, at least the idea of family, clinging to the fabric that barely held us together. Life had been simple back in those days in Los Angeles where my Mom, Dad and I lived along with several relatives in the area, while the others in our extended family lived out in Riverside. We were all so close, but not with large family gatherings, just with our love for each other.

As I have grown older and they have as well, I realize, I do love them, even those I felt have wronged the twins and I through the years, but yet, I do love them. As I think back, I was a little ragamuffin running the streets totally out of control. God only knows what would have become of me, but when our Tía Merce took control of us, we lived in a very strict household. I'm sure she saved me from God only knows what. I owe her a lot, but the twins were a different story. It breaks my heart just thinking about how they were mistreated. Yes, I love my family, some more than others but unfortunately in order to keep my sanity and live happily, I must maintain my boundaries. I do love them, but for the most part, I will only enjoy them in small dosages here and there, like a very fine expensive bottle of Scotch whiskey.

Shit, maybe that's how my dad felt about his sisters? I never thought about that. But I don't think so, maybe he treated his sisters who lived in San Diego poorly because he thought they knew what was in his heart, so he stayed away from them.

First, I want to make it clear, I'm not one to blame others for my circumstances. I take it upon myself to live a beautiful and God-filled life. My life hasn't always been perfect, but I've tried to keep my struggles private. That is the Scorpio in me. I still call myself a Catholic, if I have to call myself anything, but I am not a devout Catholic. If I attend mass every Sunday and observe all Roman Catholic holy days but walk out of church and lie, cheat, judge others and so on and so forth then it's all for show, it's all a lie. I have always considered myself a "God-fearing" woman, until one day I realized that God-Fearing meant 'devout' of which I am not, so I started thinking of other ways to describe myself. Then I thought, what the hell, I am who I am. I don't need a tagline. I have faith in my God and integrity, and I feel he is holding my hand as we explore a deeper and richer experience. Is this spirituality? Is it that different from religion? I truly believe that when the Lord calls upon me, I will go straight to heaven. My church attendance record will not hinder my entrance, but in the meantime, I feel the strength within myself, and the desire to be all I can be.

I remember how as a five-year-old, I had been praying for my mom to have a baby. I wanted twins. Being an only child was not fun. I was already five for heaven's sake, and still no brothers or sisters. Sure, I had all the attention, but I wanted a sister or brother or both like my cousins. Finally, I heard twins were on the way. Just what I had been praying for, twins! I was so excited I could hardly stand the wait. Babies don't just show up, it takes time and that is a long wait for a five-year-old who has been praying to God daily for babies.

On December 14, 1981, Mom gave birth to *los cuates* (**twins**), a green-eyed boy and a blue-eyed girl. I was so excited when we went to pick them up at the hospital and seeing the two adorable little bundles in her arms. They were so tiny, and they were my brother and sister. That's what counted. I finally had my own brother and sister. This was the best I could have asked for. It was like God had heard my prayers. They were both blond(e) and fair-complected and looked like our Dad. They were named Josefa and Francisco. Their nicknames were *Chepa* for my sister and *Pancho* for my brother, (*Chepita* and Panchito). I called them *Huera* and *Huero*. I still call them that. Huero/a is Spanish for a person of lighter complexion and light hair.

I know everyone thought their arrival would steal my thunder, but I was so excited I hadn't even given that a thought in my young five-year-old brain. I mean, it couldn't, after all, I was well-established as *La Reina de Los Ángeles*, but having a brand-new set of twins and a five-year-old *Reina de Los Ángeles* at home was a bit overwhelming for our mom.

"Mama, I can help, I can help. Let me help, Mama!" But when one cried the other cried, and when one needed attention, the other did as well. As the weeks went by, it became obvious to both my parents that all of this was just too much for my mom, and I was sent out to live with one of my mother's older sisters, my aunt Mercedes who we called Tía Merce and my Tío Rafael, and their family in Riverside.

It was exciting for me, getting to stay with my aunt and her family, but oh how I missed my mom and dad and those twins. "Tía, when will my family come to see me?" I often asked.

Riverside was like living in the country back then. My uncle worked at a dairy, so we had plenty of dairy foods, and aunt Merce raised a beef each year to butcher and feed us all. Although I missed the twins and Mom and Dad, I began to really enjoy Riverside. As I look back now, it took a bit for me to get accustomed to the structure of life in tía Merce's household. She ruled here, but I came to understand structure was good. I shared a room with my older cousin and found all of her makeup and things really intriguing. Aunt Merce enrolled me at Ina Arbuckle Elementary so I could finish out my first grade. She would walk me to the bus stop each morning. Had I been going to school in Los Angeles, I would have been walking to school with the other kids.

There was one day I will never forget. It turned out to be one of many defining moments in my young life. My cousin had already left for work when I just happened to notice that she had dropped some blush on her dresser. I just couldn't resist! I looked out the door first to be sure no one was coming, and then I got in it and rubbed it on my cheeks. I was so excited! It made me feel so grown up. Now to get out of the house without anyone seeing it, especially Tía Merce as I knew she wouldn't be happy with me. The truth be known, the blush probably wasn't even noticeable, but in the eyes of a six-year-old, it was a big deal I was sure I looked fabulous.

I heard her on the phone, knowing not to interrupt her, it was my chance.

I raced by her, waving on my way out the door, "I'm leaving, tía." That way she wouldn't see. But, outside, I panicked when I saw the bus approaching the stop across the street. If I missed it, then she would see what was on my face. I took off at a full run across the street, right out into traffic.

The next moments were blurry. I just lay there in shock. I couldn't breathe and I couldn't move. It took me a minute to realize what had just happened. I had been hit by a car. It was as if everything stopped – just stopped. I never saw the car coming, it just happened, then everything was in slow motion. Finally, I found the strength from somewhere deep to drag myself out of the road. I don't know how I did it or why. I'm assuming it was because in my state of shock, I knew I wasn't supposed to be there, or maybe that I didn't want to get hit again. From what I remember the driver said I came out of nowhere and ran out in front of her. She was shattered. And, she was not lying, that's exactly what I did.

"¡Dios mo santo, Sarita!" Tía's frantic voice was coming from somewhere, calling me, but I couldn't see her. I couldn't cry. I wanted to, I just couldn't.

"¡Dios mío Sarita!" She cried out, her voice floating through the chaos.

Andres, my neighbor and friend, had run home to tell her.

I didn't cry, I think I was too shocked and confused to cry. Finally, I looked up to see her standing over me. I could feel my eyes filling up, like a dam ready to overflow. I knew she would make everything okay, as my tears spilled down my cheeks, she gently wrapped her arms around me, fearful that any movement would hurt me more.

The ambulance and fire engines pulled up. Just seeing the firemen and the ambulance driver with a stretcher rushing towards me caused me to panic. "I'm afraid!" I gasped through my tears.

"It's okay, Sarita, it's okay." Merce whispered.

I saw her eyes filling up and ready to overflow like mine. I could see her pain as if her heart was breaking as she hesitated a moment, her hand not wanting to let go, before backing away so the men could help me.

"Please," I begged through my tears, staring into the fireman's warm, dark eyes as he brushed my long, dark hair away from my face, "Please don't take me to the hospital. My teacher will be so mad at me if I don't come to school."

"It's okay, sweetheart, no one will be mad, I promise you. But we have to get you to the hospital to fix you up again."

"You don't understand," I mumbled through my tears. "She is so mean."

He shook his head, "It will be okay. I promise"

I didn't believe him, although his voice was soft and reassuring and he tried to comfort me. The panic still rolling through me, my fear of needles blended in with all the chaos as the thought of having to have shots overtook my body. I began to shake. Obviously being hit by a car was a huge deal, no doubt I was going to get a shot or maybe a few! I have always feared needles, I don't have any tattoos or piercings other than my ears which my mother had pierced for me when I was an infant. That fear of needles made me freeze up. I felt rigid and cold. I tremble just writing this, thinking of those needles I thought would come. To this day I wonder where that fear of needles came from. They loaded me onto the ambulance and rushed me to Kaiser Hospital in Fontana. My aunt followed in the car. When we arrived, Tía Merce was beside me in no time, holding my hand so tight as if willing her strength into me through the power of her grip. They rolled me inside the big hospital.

The doctors gave me what they called a once over and said they were sending me down to x-ray so they could see the extent of the damages. I heard the nurse, speaking in Spanish to Merce.

"*Señora,* I know how hard it is, but you must sit outside the room. We have a chair out there for you. We have to get her to x-ray and then we will bring you back in when she returns." Her voice was soft, but an urgency clung in the air. This is where I lost her. She was escorted out and shown to a seat outside the room. As they wheeled me past her, I remember all the light in her face was gone. She was wiping away her tears. I started to cry again.

They rolled me and turned me this way and that. Each time asking about my pain. I hurt so bad I didn't know what hurt worse. As bad as everything looked, I was so relieved to find out there were no shots. I left the hospital that same day with a cast on my leg. I had a lot of bruises and abrasions, road rash and a broken ankle. I remember my stomach was hurting very much that night and I couldn't sleep. *Tía Merce* gave me some of her magic – a lemon with a little bit of baking soda sprinkled on top. Up came some powerful burps and my stomach pain was gone. I had to miss school for about two weeks and that was a perfect break from my horrible teacher.

I really wanted to see my mom and dad. Finally, I heard Mom was coming with the twins the weekend following the accident. I was so excited I could hardly stand it.

I stood with my crutches, with one leg in a perfect white cast other than where my cousin had signed it, and where I had drawn pictures on it, and with bruises and abrasions everywhere, just waiting for Mom. I waited and waited, and finally I saw them drive into the driveway.

She came running, her arms reaching out before she ever got to me. I will never forget her warmth and the texture of her skin. Her sweet smell.

"Sarita!" Tears flowing down her cheeks.

Her hugs were tight. I felt her love seeping in through her warmth.

"Ay mija, do you hurt anywhere?" She was crying now, as we both watched as Tía Merce carried the babies into the house. "Are you doing okay here with Merce and Rafael?"

I nodded yes. "I'm going to be okay. I miss you so much. Where is my dad?"

"He stayed home to do some work. He says for you to get well soon!"

I moved over to the couch where I could sit and hold the babies. "Mama, when can I go home?"

"Oh honey, it won't be long. Just give us some time to get the babies where they aren't so much work, and I will come and get you, I promise."

Mama came that first weekend following the accident, and then she and the twins came every two to four weeks to see me in Riverside, but my Dad never came, not once. I never once talked to either of them on the phone. Looking back now, it was so obvious that he never wanted to be around Mom's family, not ever.

CHAPTER

2ND GRADE SUCKED

"Stay in the present, Sara," I kept telling myself. The plane started bouncing around as we made our descent into Hermosillo. The stewardess came by to remind me to put my carry-on down under the seat in front of me. I did. As the plane came to a stop, I looked around to see if we were waiting for a gate. Everyone stood up but us. That's when I realized there really wasn't a gate. My brother reached for my carry-on, as I helped *Rosa* gather her things. Finally, it was our turn, we deplaned onto the tarmac, the dryness of the desert air embraced us with its freshness, and we walked towards customs. The airport was so small, I had no idea.

I tried not to show my nervousness. I took the carry-on from my brother and carried it myself. If anything was going to go sideways, I wanted to take responsibility for it. I didn't want my brother to get in trouble for something I decided to do. He gets in enough trouble on his own. I placed the bag in the container to be put through the x-ray machine and I prayed. By the grace of God, customs did not question anything. Nothing was detected. Maybe the officer checking was momentarily distracted, who knows but THANK YOU JESUS!

We stepped out into the heat of the spring day. It was quite warm. The dry desert heat worked for me. Soon, we would be in Guaymas, with more humidity, but here it was breathable and wonderful. I had only been to the state of Sonora once before, it was hot then too. I guess it is always hot here in the spring. I was shocked at the line of cabs waiting for the tourists to take them to their vacation spots.

It seems like most everyone is aware of Hermosillo, no one I know is actually from here, I thought. Only later did I discover a cousin and her husband live there. Hermosillo seems to be the place we have to go to so we can get somewhere else. I suppose the little less than a million people who live here are glad we are just passing through. My father was born further south in Sinaloa State, but not sure what town. I'm beginning to think these bits of information were never of any importance. What I do know is we have family in Los Mochis, Sinaloa, but my dad was raised in Guaymas, Sonora. And we will be there shortly.

We picked up our rental car and the three of us headed out. About a two-and-a-half-hour drive through the desert to the Sea of Cortez. The closer we got, the quieter everyone became. Not being a desert lover, I found myself strangely appreciative of the drive. That same realization of emptiness I had on the plane still clung to my edges, I just let myself absorb the desert and what appears to the human eye as emptiness but isn't at all. I wondered about myself, and how the people on the outside see me. Not that I ever really cared. Now I am beginning to question if I even know myself. Sometimes I feel this shell that everyone sees, is nothing but a hard shield to protect the fragility of my true self, and that I, nor anyone else really knows who I am. All I tell myself is I am just working my way through all the chaos, praying for some peace and joy. Someday this chaos will end.

But where will the peace and joy come from? Families come together as one, but not ours. It's split with a crevice as large as the Grand Canyon, leaving us all to pick a side as the split was too wide to straddle. But it wasn't always the Grand Canyon, or was it? Did it begin as a stream just cutting through the soft sands of relationships?

They said, they meaning my mom's sisters, that our father had a purpose in marrying our mama, but he never said that; one of my aunts said it first. She said it was to get legal citizenship. He came to the US as a boxer, he overstayed his Visa, and then he and Mama got married. All of my growing years while Mama was alive, our dad would not go anywhere near her family. He even climbed out the bedroom window once so as not to have to spend time with any of them when they came to visit.

I loved my dad and tagged along everywhere he went. Going to the gym and watching him box was awesome for me. I just wanted to be with him. He worked as a chef for the local utility company, but he loved working on cars and always seemed to be doing that in his spare time. I 'helped' him whenever I could. Being with my Dad was the best time ever for me.

One might say, I knew him better than anyone or at least I thought I did. I had five years of being alone with him before the twins came. Those were five years of pure joy, at least of all I could remember. On weekends we would include Mom and go to the beach or to some of the theme parks, life was good.

There were days, Mama and I would get on a bus and go around to different places, it was fun, but never as exciting as with Dad. Now, looking back, it all leaves me wondering if I ever knew my father. Did anyone know him? Does anyone know my brother and sister since they have become adults? Does anyone know me? How many people walk around thinking this?

Mexico seemed to bring *mi papi,* closer to me. It was stirring up the memories of my childhood, but there was a lot more to my childhood than those first five years, which were always the good times, but that was before the twins were born. I glanced over at my brother, Huero. A man now, always known to our parents as *Francisco,* to the rest of the world as *Pancho,* but to me as *Huero.* He too has grown into a troubled man I no longer know, and I could feel the tightness in my chest, the fear of what he might tell me when we are alone. I thought of *Josefa,* his twin, the family all called her *Chepa* or *Chepita* when she was younger. I have always called her *Huera.* I was so excited when they were born, I had no idea what life was going to deal us. The trauma these two babies carried into adulthood is more than should be expected of any child. We told *Huera* we were coming down with our Dad's ashes, but she expressed no interest.

Who are we, how did we come to be who we are today? I wonder, I wonder, I wonder. They had their first five years with Mom and Dad too, but things were changing. The only thing that didn't change was Mom's love for them and how she spoiled them. Which, by all rights, I was spoiled, too. It was what Mom did. I didn't know it until much later that our dear mother had been diagnosed with bipolar when she was 15, and I don't remember much about that before the twins came along, and maybe it was the stress of having the two babies in the house and a busy five-year-old, which was me, that caused her to start having the episodes. I don't know. I don't think anyone knows, but I didn't like it when they happened. It was terrifying how she changed so fast.

Rosa began to stir in the passenger seat. "Why does this seem like such a long drive?"

"I was just thinking," I spoke up, "did you enjoy growing up down here, or did you actually grow up in Los Mochis?"

"Our family, your family, the family, however we want to say it, we were from Sinaloa but like your Dad, we were raised up here. It will feel good to be home."

Home, I thought, mulling over the word. Home has so many different meanings. The American slang, "Home is where you hang your hat" which means wherever you happen to be living at the moment or "Home is where the heart is". For some, it is the house in which they grew up and their parents still live in it. Many people bond with their surroundings and that to them is where their heart is, so it is home. I think it is the familiarity of a time when things were simpler. I could only imagine the free spirit of the Baja that made them so happy. The gentleness of the Sea of Cortez. Gentle memories.

Those thoughts were surfacing again as I realized, I do wonder who I really am. It is almost like I am of two different cultures. My memories are split between before the spring of '87 and after the spring of '87. If I want to get a little more precise, we can break the before into before the twins were born and after they were born. No wonder I feel fractured. Even before the spring of '87 there was no blending of our families. Lots of people have family from one country and family from another, why do I feel so different? Could it be that because we are Mexican on both sides of the family, that we are expected to be one big happy family wrapped in the arms of the Catholic Church? Where did this thought come from? Why did this family never blend like other families? I realize now, that just because we are all Mexican and Catholic doesn't mean we are the same. In order to understand who, I am, we have to understand who they were.

Mama was the baby sister in the family of four older sisters and four brothers, all my aunts and uncles. Her sisters, like her, were all born in Mexico's central-western State of Jalisco, in the beautiful little town of Juchitlán.

Mama was beautiful, and it was in a simpler time. They were raised with such strictness of love and fear of their religion, that no one even thought of breaking away from the Church or divorcing.

My dad was raised further north in Guaymas, Sonora, where like so many young men in those days, he worked on fishing boats, and everybody ate lots of fish. To a young nine-year-old, when my Dad brought me down here to visit his family, the one thing that struck me was everyone only ate flour tortillas. Mom's family came from much further south, and they only ate corn tortillas, unless it was to be used to make a burrito, then they used flour. This may make you laugh, but the tortillas were the one thing I noticed, and it stuck with me all these years, and it was only the beginning of the differences. Tradition is rich in Mexican culture, and some things are just the way they are. Sonoran cuisine is known to be much milder than the Border cuisine that we are all used to, and the further south, the milder the food. Plus, being on the coast, the seafood is plentiful, and its cuisine is chock full of its deliciousness.

And then there were the accents when they spoke. Dad always spoke differently than Mom and her family and when I got down to Sonora and Sinaloa, everyone spoke like my dad. It was one of those "Oh my gosh" moments. The accents are so different, it was like having part of our family from Boston and the other part from west Texas and Oklahoma.

Familiar landscapes take one on a journey in itself into our inner thoughts, into our subconscious mind. And now I am thinking of the flour tortillas vs the corn tortillas. The tortilla preferences of these two families are just the beginning. The only thing they have in common is their Mexican heritage. From there on it's crazy. Mom's side of the family, most of whom were raised in California are about as devout Catholics as anyone on the planet. They are right up there with the Pope. Extremely strict, and God forbid if any of them had a baby out of wedlock. Whoa! That was really bad in this family, at least back in the day. It was all very hush-hush and absolutely frowned upon. It still is. The strictness in the way they were raised made sure of this. Whereas in my dad's family, none of this mattered. They too are Catholics, but the word "devout" cannot be used in referring to that side of the family. Sure, they attend mass when they want to, especially on Christmas and Easter, but whereas my mom's side went to mass on Sundays, and also during the week. No wonder the Grand Canyon seems like a fair analogy when I think of the vastness of the split as the years went on. I really need to address this fractured feeling.

But let's understand, after becoming so aware of this difference, as I got older, I finally realized how this tortilla issue came to be. The state of Sonora had great luck growing wheat, therefore the flour tortillas, but further south where our mother and her relatives all came from, their success was with corn. This difference wasn't so sinister. It was a natural flow of farming. I remember how happy it made me to discover the difference in the tortillas was something so logical.

This was more 'deep thinking' than I had done forever. As we came over the rise, the first view of the Sea of Cortez was stunning, what a welcome relief to my eyes. I wanted to pull off and just soak it in. I could feel it reach out to my heart and bring me out of my trance. Such a gorgeous blue. Pulling off just to think didn't seem plausible with my brother and aunt Rosa in the car. I continued driving as Rosa came alive the closer we got. Her excitement did make me more understanding of her thoughts of home.

"Oh look!" she exclaimed. "Kids look at the water! It is absolutely beautiful. This time of the day was always my favorite time down here. Midafternoon, the sun starts reaching towards the west, shining back through the water. Oh my God, how I love it here. If we were close to the church right now, you would see it bathed in that glow."

Huero, who had been sleeping all the way, woke up and leaned into the front area to face Rosa, "tell us, what did you do all day when you were kids growing up here? Was it a fun place to live?"

I looked over at him, it was the most he had said at one time during the whole trip.

"It was beautiful here. It wasn't as built up as it is now, but the church was always here, in fact our church has been here for over a hundred years or more. Always beautiful. We played in the streets, and there were lots of open beaches in those days. You could see for miles. There is something very relaxing about living around the water. Sure, we had our share of storms, but they were nothing like living on the Pacific side. The Sea of Cortez is quite protected, not totally, but quite." Her voice trailed off.

I made a left and headed south following Rosa's directions, toward Tía Sara's home, wondering why *Rosa* had never moved back here. She had been living in San Diego for as long as I could remember. Maybe I will ask later. As we entered the main part of town, we first dropped off *Rosa* at her sister's. I got out of the car and helped her with her bag, then gave them each a hug. "We'll pick you up about 5:00 p.m. and that will give us a little time and we can be there to greet the others as they arrive."

"I'm assuming that's the plan, right?" I said, "whoever will be attending will meet us there?" Just trying to make sure we had all of this straight.

Tía Sara, still with her arms around me, agreed, but did mention we would be very early, as Rosa reached in for another hug. They both clung to me, maybe just a moment longer than I had expected. They had been kept from me for years when I was little, through our failing family dynamics. Now I wondered could that warmth actually be the real love they had been wanting to share all those years or was it just their sadness of the day.

My brother and I drove on through town to the hotel, right on the water, to get checked in. The private mass was scheduled for 7:00 p.m. and then to the cemetery at ten tomorrow morning. I was a little apprehensive about the cemetery visit, not knowing what to expect, but first let's get through the mass, I told myself. Then I can deal with this. I looked at my watch, just a few minutes past two.

I had set my mind to the fact that tonight and tomorrow would be the beginning of the end of this phase of my life. But now, I wasn't so sure. I was becoming more aware by the moment that yes, I have to come to grips with all of this, but this too is a part of who I am. Maybe. For God's sake, I'm 35 years old and I have been dealing with this for 25 years. I was determined to put all of this behind me and move forward. I like tying knots and being done with something. Closure, but for some reason, this doesn't feel like closure. I am not so sure I even know what this feeling is.

I thought about that extra moment of warmth from them. That feeling lingered as I unlocked the hotel door, and walked into the coolness, shutting the door behind me. I was glad I was alone. The room smelled a bit musty. I scanned the darkness of the room, and then, eyes adjusting, I went to the sliding patio doors, pulled open the curtains and opened the doors wide and just stood there soaking in the fresh sea breeze and the beautiful sunshine. Large families have their place in the world and in our hearts, but it also is important for people to spend time alone. In this moment of aloneness, I needed to gather myself, the emptiness had spread through my soul. *Papi* and the murder of *my mom* and the abuse of the twins had taken up all I had for so long, and with this huge part of it all,

coming to an end with his passing, I am not surprised at this emptiness. Not surprised at all – it has been who I am, my being for most
of my life. I feel dry inside.

I was still wrestling with the idea of my empty heart and soul
filling up with all I had missed through the years. Am I too cynical
to ever let the bygones pass or has all the trauma ingrained itself
into my every pore? I was just beginning to see everything more
clearly. What I was seeing, scared me.

I had waited long enough from the time my Dad died to now,
and at the beginning, I worried my lack of emotion would be evi-
dent while with his family. I had always believed that I felt nothing,
and it really scared me. How could I become so hardened as to not
show the emotion of his passing and bringing him to his final resting
place? But recognizing this feeling of "nothing" as really emptiness,
just empty, when it truly is filled with life. Is that an excuse, I wondered, for my lack of emotions? How did what started out to be so
promising end up so empty? I'm just doing my duty. I thought it
was the right thing to do, then I can get on with my life. That was
the plan, now I am wondering if there is more to all of this than I
have led myself to believe. Unfamiliar feelings were coming to the
surface. This mass was to be in Spanish and to be for his family here
in Mexico, and to bury his ashes alongside his mother in her casket.

I noticed that I keep doing things for others, the first mass was
for his San Diego friends, now this one was a private mass for his
family. What about me, what about my brother? Do we not count?
Why am I not considering us in the family? Why are we, even in my
own mind, always on the edge, never embraced as family? God, I
thought I had all of this figured out, just get it done, get it over with,
and get on with my life. I am so confused.

I had migrated to the deck chair out on the little patio off my
room. I thought of the day I was hit by the car and being so afraid.

Was I more afraid of my teacher being angry with me for not coming to school than I was of the hospital? The accident had gotten me a few weeks out of school which made me really happy, as I didn't like my second-grade teacher at all. Her name was Mrs. Cabrera. She was probably the meanest teacher I ever had. She even pulled my ear one day! Anyone that attended Ina Arbuckle will know exactly who she is. My goodness, I'd love to run into her now that I'm a grown woman and remind her what she did and how it felt.

Back then it was different, discipline was a lot more physical. Nowadays she would have lost her job.

I'm pretty sure Mrs. Cabrera has retired by now but seven years ago she was still teaching. Still at Ina Arbuckle Elementary, teaching 1st grade. My best friend called me one day asking if she could use my address because she wanted to move her daughter to the school by my house. Her daughter was starting 1st grade and on the first day of school, my friend saw the teacher grab her daughter by her arm and place her in another place in line. She said she was very rough and rude. I said, "Really? Shit! Who is this teacher manhandling little six-year-old girls?"

She said her name is Mrs. Cabrera. Oh, my gawd! That bitch is still alive and well I see. I can't imagine that my friend's daughter and I were the only little girls she put her hands on. That lady was something else. I'm sure at some point, there had to be a parent that complained. But, on the other hand, Ina Arbuckle is on the worst side of town, a very ghetto area and maybe that's why parents did not complain or did not know how to make their voices heard at the school district.

Like some of the teachers, parents were a lot more hands-on, sometimes excessively. I'll never forget what happened in first grade. There was a little girl my age named Ursula who apparently was a nuisance in the classroom. I was a new girl and had not been around enough to notice or she really wasn't that bad. Evidently, my teacher at the new school, Ms. Lopez, had contacted her mother complaining of her daughter's behavioral problems in the classroom. One morning, Ursula's mother walked into the classroom with a leather belt in her hand. She walked up to Ursula, ordered her to stand and in front of all the children and Ms. Lopez, she proceeded to whip Ursula five times with the belt on her rear. Everyone watched in disbelief. Ursula cried and I felt her pain. I thought, "Ooooh no, she didn't just hit her?" I will never forget Ursula's face. God bless her.

I was not physically disciplined by my parents very often. I think Mom did most of the disciplining, but it was mostly verbal. Whatever physical discipline she gave me was not significant. I have no recollection of it. *Mi papi* never yelled at me, he was very calm and patient but there is one time I will never forget. I had spent the afternoon with my cousin, Rosa, Rosarita Refried Beans which was what I always called her. She, and some of my cousins call me Sara Lee, like the pastries, it must be my sweetness. I came home wearing some bright shade of lipstick that I probably got from my cousin's room. I walked into my house feeling as fierce and fabulous as is possible for a eight-year-old until my dad said,

"Why are you wearing that on your face? You're too young for makeup. Please go clean your face."

I turned around and as I walked away, I told him, "I'll wear it if I want to, it's my life, not yours."

I was eight years old of all things, and I still don't know what made me feel it was okay to speak to my father in that manner. Maybe the lipstick gave me a false sense of reality and I thought I was 30 years old? My father brought me back to reality quick by way of three very painful spanks that I will never forget. That is the only physical form of discipline I remember and the only time.

After being away from home for over a year, I was no longer thrilled about living in Riverside. I really wanted my mother. I missed her dearly. Eventually, my parents purchased a home in East Los Angeles, Boyle Heights to be exact, and I moved back in with them. That was one of the happiest days of my life, coming back home to Los Angeles with my parents and the twins. I had not seen my dad since I had been sent to live with tía Merce in Riverside. Now, I was seven years old and a 2nd grader at Euclid Elementary School.

Being a new girl at school was not fun. Every day we were sent to a different classroom for language arts. Once again, I got stuck with an awful teacher named Corazon Aquino. Ms. Aquino was very mean, but not as mean as Mrs. Cabrera, she was the worst. School in East Los Angeles was different than school in Riverside. First of all, in East Los Angeles, we were mostly all Latino. I remember the first time I saw the kids in Riverside, fifth and sixth graders walking around holding hands, like couples. Wearing lipstick and other makeup. In LA, our parents were strict, and we were never allowed makeup or boyfriends in elementary school.

School was walking distance from my home and the Euclid campus was not as secured as Ina Arbuckle campus had been. Although Ms. Aquino was not nearly as bad as Mrs. Cabrera, I couldn't stand going to her classroom. She had an awful face, and she never smiled. I remember thinking how terrible it would be to be her daughter. I don't know why I had that thought, other than she was so cold. She had what we now know as a "resting bitch face". She was also very arrogant and intimidating. She spoke with a heavy Filipino accent and to me, looked like Roz, one of the characters from the movie Monsters Inc.

One day, I decided I'd had enough of her. I no longer was going to deal with her, and I was going to do something about it. I raised my hand and asked for permission to go to the restroom. Ms. Aquino told me to go and hurry back. I thought, *hurry back, yeah, right lady, whatever.* I left the classroom and walked off campus. I walked about one mile to my aunt Socorro's (we called her tía *Soco*) house with every intention of watching cartoons. Thunder Cats was my favorite, by the way.

Surprised by my visit in the middle of the day, "What are you doing here, Sarita? Why are you not in school?" Tía Soco asked.

I told her the truth. I explained I was unhappy with Ms. Aquino, and I wanted nothing to do with her.

She looked at me and simply said, "*Ay Sarita*" (**"Oh Sarita"**).

Tía Soco was another of my mother's sisters. She lived on Fresno Street, about a mile and a half away from my house which was located on South Dacotah Street. The I-5 separated our neighborhoods. I'm not sure what crossed her mind, but she let me stay and did not call my mother, big mistake.

I had been enjoying my self-granted day for about two hours when the police came knocking on the door and to top it off my mother was with them. Oh man, I was in deep trouble, not with the policeman, but with my mother. She had sprained her ankle that morning, and she had really struggled to walk me to school. I literally added insult to injury by walking off campus after she had put so much effort into getting me there safely. I learned very young how to assert my independence, but it didn't always work. Aunt Soco and I both learned from this, and I never did it again.

On a lighter note, after all the shenanigans, I did get an opportunity to formally complain about the stress Ms. Aquino was bringing to my life. As a result, I no longer had to attend her class for language arts. *Even when it's bad it's good!*

CHAPTER 3

CIRCA '84/'85

As the sea breeze brushed across my face, I took a deep breath. I love it here. I could just see myself when I was little and visiting my dad's family here. I felt so special that I got to come. There was more to that year than just our trip to visit dad's family. The school year, 1984-1985 was quite an eventful year. It unfolded in an array of startling things. I started 3rd grade at a new school in East LA, Sunrise Elementary. We, the City of Los Angeles, hosted the 1984 Olympics while many in the greater LA area were in a panic while Richard Ramirez "The Night Stalker" ran amuck. He was killing, raping, and burglarizing the residents of the greater Los Angeles area from June 1984 until August 1985 when he was arrested on Hubbard Street in East LA. So, needless to say it was a time of many events in my life. One might think an eight-year-old would not be concerned about a killer running loose, but it became the topic of conversation in every household and at every dinner table. And we heard a lot about Russia that year, as they boycotted our Olympics. So those, and a new school, which I was praying for nice teachers, and teachers that smiled, then Dad said he was taking me with him to visit his family in Mexico. I was over-the-moon with excitement.

I couldn't help but wonder, as I have so many times before, where did we lose our dad? When did I lose him? Or did I ever really have him? Did we ever really know him? Our trip down here was on a bus, and I remember I whined a lot. It was something about being so confined plus the road at the time was a very narrow two-lane road and had some huge drop-offs. It terrified me. I was so busy being unhappy about this ride that seemed to go on forever, that I had never really thought about how my dad was responding to the trip. But looking back now, I remember how quiet he was, and wonder if his thoughts had him questioning why he ever left home for good. Coming back home to see his mother and his family, maybe he was a bit sorry he had ever left.

"Dad, when will we get there?" This was the furthest I had been from home. Getting to go visit his family was a fun idea, but I was not prepared for the long and scary bus ride. My pent-up energy had me tied in knots and I was terrified until we got close to the water, and I came alive just like my relatives from the past. The water. I couldn't wait to be in the water, and I knew he would take me swimming, as he had taught me how. I was so excited.

That bus ride has stuck in my memory forever as one of many terrible experiences in my life. It wouldn't scare me now but as an eight-year-old, oh my God – one of the most terrifying experiences in my young life. La Rumorosa, have you been on that road? Back in the day, it was the route the busses took to get to Sonora and to this day it is known as the most dangerous road in all of Mexico, and I can tell you there are several that come close to that designation. La Rumorosa is actually a mountain pass in the Sierra Juarez and tops out at 4,042 feet. It is filled with an overwhelming amount of curves and hairpin turns and lots of dips. And, I wonder to this day if they have ever put guardrails up. Linking the cities of Tecate and Mexicali, I didn't like it then, and I'm sure I wouldn't like it now. I'm terrified of heights and this was just too much. I always felt the bus was going to go over the edge. So maybe this soured me on buses as well, but I do understand why so many take the bus, even to this day. Since rental cars are so expensive, that mode of travel is pretty much out of reach for the locals, and buses are inexpensive, and they run at all times. Those who know Mexico, the locals, feel bus travel is much safer. It protects them from a more aggressive harassment while crossing the border, and it actually is a carefree way for the locals to travel back and forth.

Other than the bus ride, I have really delightful memories of that trip with my dad. It was wonderful to meet his family and, in a space where he had grown up. Dad was so different while we were there. He was happy, which made me realize later on, that I had never known him to be happy. That's a strange thought. He took me all over, showing me all the places a normal tourist would never see. He even took me down to the fishing boats. He knew a lot of people down there that he used to work with, and he seemed proud to introduce me to them all. As we wandered the streets, many people remembered him. It was the happiest time I can remember, seeing him with his family, laughing and just being home. My father adored his mother and he sent her money every paycheck and he purchased her home, he called her once a week, back then that was a lot especially since he called her from a pay phone. He always took care of her. He was a momma's boy for sure. I hope my sons think of me as much as my father did about his momma when they finally move out.

But of all the things that stuck in my mind, nothing could match the kitchens and the food and family. This really made for some fond memories for this eight-year-old. My favorite was caldo de queso. It was such a delicious soup we had one late afternoon for our supper.

Even to this day, I make it for my family, but it never quite tastes the same, and I am just assuming it is because we can't get the *queso de rancho Sonorense* – *a* Sonoran cheese that they used down there. Machaca was another, we all love burritos, but when you have them with dried beef, it makes a world of difference. And then came the coyotas, and what eight-year-old doesn't like cookies, and truth be known, there aren't many dads out there either who don't like cookies. These were special, they were the ones my *papi* grew up with, more like a turnover and they were delicious.

Although our family has been blessed with good cooks all the way around, it tasted even more wonderful here where it had originated. It seemed to flow like the water, things were because they were. Looking back there was a different sense of being here. At home, our family prepared a few traditional dishes, like tamales, enchiladas, and Turkey at Christmas, but they also did a lot of "American-style" cooking, like meatloaf, and a lot of hamburger dishes.

That fall, I was a fourth grader. I hadn't had a lot of luck with good teachers, so I was a bit apprehensive. But when Ms. Iniguez walked into our room, I knew I was one lucky little girl. I loved Ms. Iniguez so much, she was the best teacher I had ever had. She went above and beyond, she spent personal time with me. She was an artist and art was something I really enjoyed. I had the opportunity to go to her home and work on different art projects. Our School District had a short story writing contest which she encouraged me to enter. I did but then I stressed over the whole process. I was happy with the outcome and received an award for my story. My mother was very proud, which pleased me.

Another little girl and I were chosen for a shopping spree at the local Pic-N-Save some of you old timers might remember that discount store. To a little East LA girl that was a memorable experience, and I loved every minute of it.

I once asked Ms. Iniguez how she became an artist as we sat at her desk.

She thought for a minute, and then responded, "We are all artists because we were all born with a special God-given talent and it was up to us to explore our creativity in an effort to discover what our special talent is," she said. "Anything we enjoy doing that makes another person smile is an art. Dancing, writing, drawing, makeup, singing, teaching are all forms of art, and we should enjoy our lives by sharing our artistic creativity."

Ms. Iniguez would have a Sausage Egg McMuffin and a coffee for breakfast every morning. She said she couldn't share because it was very expensive and not a good breakfast for children. I believed her and I thought, when I grow up, I'm going to make a lot of money so I can have a Sausage Egg McMuffin with a coffee for breakfast every morning like her. Now, if you have spent any quality time with me as an adult, you know my go-to breakfast is a Sausage McMuffin with a small coffee and 5 creams and 5 Splendas.

My heart feels warm just remembering this wonderful woman, ahhh, Ms. Iniguez, the things you taught me. When I told her how wonderful she smelled, she told me it's Paloma Picasso. That was the perfume she wore and then she told me that Paloma was the daughter of the famous artist, Pablo Picasso. And, then I learned all about the Picassos. To this day, I wear that same perfume or one that smells so much like it. I always love to smell wonderful. Another thing was how she read to us each day. Judy Blume and Shel Silverstein were the two authors she read to us most of the time, and today I read books because she taught me the joys of reading and I own a small collection of Shel Silverstein books. Although I have a career in law enforcement, I became a professional makeup artist because of her inspiring words.

Even in all my shyness, I opened up to her a bit about the issues my mother was having, because I was being bullied by a girl in school who was making ugly remarks about my Mom. There were a lot of times my mom would do embarrassing things when she was on one of her episodes, maybe I just had to vent. Who knows but I'll never forget Ms. Iniguez's response. She said, "Sara, your mother is a strong beautiful woman and she loves you very much don't ever forget that." That's all I needed to hear – it made me feel so much better. Ms. Iniguez was there for me. She also ripped that little girl a new one and told her exactly what she thought about bullies. Teachers, when they are engaged with their students, are worth more than their weight in gold. Looking back now, I believe God was speaking to me, comforting me through her. She always complimented me in class but she did it masterfully, students did not think I was being treated special. That woman was such an impact on my life, I wish I could find her and tell her how amazing she was and how I have always held onto her encouragement. Her words guided me through some of the trials and tribulations of my life. Words of affirmation are free, being kind is free and can affect a person tremendously. Be kind to a child, an adult, or a homeless person – just fucking be kind! I wish my siblings saw a little more kindness in their childhood, I wish I was more kind to them when they were little also. I think older siblings do tend to be a little mean to the younger siblings at times, but the last thing the twins needed was an asshole sister to pick on them. I fucked up and sometimes wasn't as nice as I should have been with my siblings. There is no excuse. I recognize it and regret it now. But with all that said I hope I can be a positive role model in someone's life like Ms. Iniguez was for me.

Life in East LA was full of freedom. We roamed the streets, played outside, fought at times when it seemed the right thing to do, we had our own agenda, and we were not afraid. We bought ice cream from the *paletero* (**ice cream man**) who was a naughty old man. We had to watch ourselves around him because he had some quick hands if you know what I mean. We were scrappy little kids exposed to constant danger, but we were oblivious to that reality. The ghetto bird (**police helicopter**) was almost a nightly routine but as far as I was concerned, my life was perfect. I was a happy ten-year-old little girl.

CHAPTER 4

HE CHANGED
AND SOMETHING
TRIGGERED HER

We always like to say times were different back then, but I wonder. When I think of domestic violence, I don't really relate it to anything I had heard about in my young life, but then again, people didn't talk about it in the open like they do now. It was stashed away with other family secrets. And, we have a lot of them. I guess all families do. Thinking back, trying to make all of this make sense somehow, I can see how our home wasn't filled with an abundance of love, but I can't recall any incident where my parents were physically or verbally abusive towards each other. Maybe they were really good at hiding it? As an adult, and after a twenty-year marriage, and twenty years in law enforcement, I know for a fact, there are times when it gets pretty unpleasant. I've heard stories from my aunts, but I don't remember anything that I can define as domestic violence. I had a great relationship with both of my parents. I loved my dad; in my eyes he was the best. Honestly, I only have good memories of him, until the day the memories stopped. I loved my mom. Just being with her, no matter what we were doing, was fun and I loved her warmth and her beautiful smile. Dad taught me how to swim, how to fish off the Santa Monica Pier at night, he taught me how to love the music of Pedro Infante, Invasores de Nuevo Leon, Cadetes de Linares, Geardo Reyes and all Northern Regional Mexican music that I still listen to today. He was a big fan of Golden Age of Mexican cinema actors Pedro Infante, Maria Felix and Silvia Pinal because they were Sonora and Sinaloa natives. Silvia Pinal was born in Guaymas, his little one horse town, and he was very proud of that. I enjoyed him very much. Every Saturday morning, I would go with him, he would buy *La Opinion*, the Spanish newspaper, and a *caguama* a (**tall boy/32 oz beer**) for him, and a bag of corn nuts and a juice for me. Then he would find a place to park under a tree somewhere and he would read his paper while I sat there and did nothing. I loved it. There were times when I would invite myself and he didn't really want to take me like when he went jogging.

Still to this day, jogging has never been "my thing" but I wanted to go with him anyway.

"No Sarita! You don't like it. You're going to get tired; you're going to get mad and plant yourself on the ground and I'm going to end up carrying you home."

"No, Dad, I won't. I promise." I would say, but, of course, I'd get tired, throw a fit, and he would carry me back home.

Dad was light skinned, his hair more a rich brown tone, but had a lot of red pigmentation in it. His name was Felipe Paredes. He always had a short haircut, and it was curly, a soft curl which set off his sparkling brown eyes. He didn't have a mustache or a beard but when he didn't shave for a few days, enough to grow a little more than a 5 o'clock shadow, the growth would be a light red. He always wore a white skipper hat from his days fishing in Guaymas.

He loved the ocean; he would often take us fishing and to the beach and to the swimming pool where he taught me how to swim. He always ran and lifted weights also did punching bag exercises. He would go up and down in weight with the belly, but he was not a fat or skinny man, not very tall, about 5'10" and no tattoos. He came to the United States on a Boxing Athletic Visa at 19, handsome and very athletic, He was 28 years old when he met and married my mom. He did make his living with boxing when he first came to the US because he was a fulltime athlete but I'm not sure how long that lasted. By the time he married our mother he was no longer boxing. He worked as a chef for the LA Department of Water and Power. He also fixed cars. I suppose it was his hobby, but boxing was what he enjoyed the most. He also loved baseball but did not play. Boxing was a part of his life until he died. Because he had been a boxer, he served as a referee at small boxing events. He spent a lot of time in boxing gyms and knew a lot of people in the boxing world. These were events I would invite myself to and he would, mostly against his will, take me. I loved it! Boxing is still one of my favorite sports.

At other times, he fixed cars, and I would sit outside "helping" him. I was a little girl, but I knew a lot about car parts and tools. I learned from listening to him place orders at the auto parts store or hearing him talk with his friends who would stand around while he did the mechanic thing. If we were alone, he would teach me about the different parts and what each function was. He would say things like *"pasame la llave de tuercas"* (pass me the lug wrench.) I knew a lot more about cars at nine years old than I do now. Fueling up my vehicle is about as far as my vehicle mechanical talents go now and even that is hard for me to do but it's all good. I've got AAA on speed dial.

I searched back for memories of my mom. She was beautiful by anyone's standards. She was a little on the heavy side, but her hourglass figure was the envy of many. She was definitely what is known now as "bootylicious". What I remember most was her smile and her warmth I felt in her presence, even as a child. Riding the bus around downtown LA was great fun and she was fun to be with, very social, a total extrovert. The two of us loved going to the juice bar at Grand Central Market and, the other thing we loved doing together was watching all the good sitcoms from back in the day like *I Love Lucy, Gilligan's Island,* and *I Dream of Jeannie*. We spent a lot of time with Tía Carmen, who was the oldest sibling in my mother's family. Carmen always had food for my mom and helped her a lot with financial assistance. I understand now, this was because our father would send money to his mom and little sister in Mexico. They came first it seems. Carmen was an awesome lady who passed away several years ago. She had been one of my many devout Catholic ties. I think that's great! I hope all who are still with us will pray for me.

My mom kept me busy. She enrolled me in different activities. I remember doing ceramics and dance classes. I was on the drill team, and she taught me how to crochet and cross-stitch embroidery. And she always volunteered at my school. Because I was an only child for five years, both of my parents spent a lot of quality time with me. Before the twins came along, we were always out and about every weekend at Knotts Berry Farm, Disneyland or the beach. What I wouldn't give for those days back again, and I still wonder where it all went wrong.

Things weren't always perfect for me though in my small five-year-old world. They bought me a bike and roller skates, but they weren't anything close to what I thought a five-year-old, the Queen of Los Angeles, should be using. My parents took me to Fedco, off of La Cienega to buy my bike. I had my heart set on a pink Strawberry Shortcake bike like every other girl wanted. I was no different, I really wanted that bike, but my parents didn't see it that way, and I ended up with an ugly blue bike with a banana seat. Ugh!! it was awful looking but my dad gave me some excuse as to why the blue bike was much better than my fabulous pink Strawberry Shortcake bike.

For the life of me, I couldn't understand this at all, and I was not happy. I set my bottom lip out, and made sure they saw it, and I never said a word the whole way home. I was so angry with them. They had never done this to me before. My heart was broken. I couldn't even imagine me riding that thing. My anger was aimed at both of them – Dad for buying that ugly blue bike and Mom for letting me down. She let me down! I thought what is wrong with these two. What are they thinking?! Blue is for boys, and I am a girl! Not only that, at the time of my bike purchase they still had me convinced I was a queen. Queens don't ride ugly boy bikes. I was setting my sites on finding new parents. They are not treating me like a queen! They don't love me. I was fuming.

Then I got my first pair of roller skates, again from Fedco, again my parents bought me the most hideous pair they found. I went home very unhappy and with an awful looking pair of roller skates. The bootie part was red and the wheels were yellow. All I could think was they looked like El Chapulin Colorado (*The Red Grass-hopper*) roller skates. El Chapulin Colorado was a Mexican sitcom. An antagonistic representation of a superhero; he was goofy and created more problems than he solved. He wore a red and yellow costume and did not wear roller skates but if he did, my roller skates would have been ideal. After a few days, I gave in to my roller skates and they took me out to a parking lot by our house to practice. Both of my parents helped me learn to roller skate and to this day I still get down on roller skates, just saying.

Sitting here watching the sun glisten on the water like silver threads as far as I can see, the sea breeze still caressing my face, I realize how spoiled I was. My heart really struggles with going back to when the twins were born, and how the dynamics in our lives changed forever. No one wanted the twins more than I did. I had been praying for at least a year for a baby sister or brother, or twins. Twins would be good. From the moment I heard we had twins on the way, my excitement was ramped up twenty-fold. And to think those two tiny little innocent bundles of joy, how their presence was able to change things so dramatically and how the added stress affected our mom. No, don't get me wrong, I am not blaming the babies for any of this. It is just how things unraveled at the time.

After I moved back home, my little family never really was the same again. Dad was different, withdrawn. He spent a lot more time with his best friend who we called *El Paisa* or *El Paisano* (country or the countryman). That is a term used amongst folks that come from the same origin. *El Paisano* was our neighbor. He and his girlfriend, Lupe, lived two houses away. Lupe was a seamstress who made dresses for my mom and aunts. I was too young as it was happening, but looking back now, I can remember there were times when my mom would act differently. Now we know she was bipolar.

Like a lot of people diagnosed with this, she refused to take her medication as prescribed. She would have short cycles of elevated or depressed mood swings. It happened in episodes, occasionally, maybe twice or three times a year, or at least that's how I remember it. I remember her acting really strange, now I would describe it as bizarre and bellicose. It was a situation that I understand now, but being ten, these things were beyond my comprehension. All I knew is that she would change. She was rude and downright mean to certain people. Never towards the twins or me, although one night in the middle of the night, she woke me up and took me outside for no reason. She was pulling my arm in a very harsh manner. It must have been after 5 a.m. because my dad was not home. He had probably already left for work. Had he been home, he would never have let her treat me that way. I have no clue what triggered her but she had to be out of her mind in that moment. She made me kneel outside the back door I don't know why? It was like she was punishing me for something. I don' t remember all that she was telling me but she was not being herself. She left me out there for what seemed like a long time. I don' t remember how long. I don't remember if she let me back in or if I let myself in. I think I wanted to forget that awful moment so desperately that I suppressed the memory and it's almost all gone. I remember feeling scared outside in the cold and darkness. I wonder if any neighbors heard or saw what was going on. I feared for my mom when she had her episodes because I was afraid she was going to get herself in trouble one day, hurt or arrested or maybe it was my subconscious warning me of what was coming, how she really was getting herself into trouble, the ultimate most horrifying trouble that would subsequently end her life.

It was with other family members she would display such anger. I thought something had happened to trigger her responses. Maybe my dad did something that would upset her. Maybe it just happened when she encountered a stressful situation. That was one of the reasons I was sent to Riverside not long after the twins were born, a busy five-year-old would only add stress to my mother's life while she was dealing with the two newborn babies. She didn't neglect us when she had an episode, she still fed us and we were cared for, but I did not like it. As I look back on her behavior, it was mortifying but I knew it would only last a few days and I would have her back, the real version of her.

CHAPTER

5

1987

We had a cold start to spring in Los Angeles that year with lots of drizzle, and then spring literally burst into full bloom. It seemed everyone was ready for it. It ranged in the 70s, perfect for life and love and children and all things wonderful. People out riding their bikes, laying out in the welcome sunshine at the beach. There were possibilities everywhere one looked. Life was good!

But at our little house, things were becoming more difficult. The twins were now five, and very busy little ones and Mom had them spoiled, spoiled, spoiled. They pretty much did whatever they wanted to do, even eating in the bedroom, and bouncing on the beds. They were her joys. I was ten. One would have thought we made it past the rough stage, but our dad was pulling away from us and our mom had been acting strange again, and it seemed to be more pronounced, or else I was older now and paying more attention.

After living with tía Merce and her family for over a year, I had a better idea about how life should be. Her structure and the respect they showed for each other always comes to the forefront, although at ten, I don't think I would have used the word 'respect' – I think maybe that was love I was feeling among the family members. I was an outsider, but overall, they included me in their family. Now, back in Los Angeles, I had something to judge or compare, when our lives felt like the cement that holds family together was crumbling.

Our mom had been having one of her episodes for a few days, and she had left to go somewhere early that Saturday morning. Dad walked into my room. I couldn't say he was angry, but he was visibly stressed, probably over Mom's actions.

"Sarita, pack some clothes for you and the twins because I am taking you kids to Riverside for a few days. And hurry, before your mother comes back, or she won't let you go."

Wow, I was super excited because this meant I didn't have to go to school. Apparently, he had already called tía Merce and made the arrangements. This would be something new for the twins, they had never been away from our mother. I rushed around and helped them dress, and we were on our way.

We pulled into her driveway.

Dad said, "You kids stay here, and I will be right back to get you. I need to talk to your Tía Merce for a minute."

That alone was strange, as we always piled out to wrap our arms around her. But then again, it was strange that my Dad was even going to talk to her, as this wasn't his normal way.

He returned to the car, gave the twins and me a hug, and was gone. I said goodbye to my Dad not knowing that I wouldn't see him, not even once, for about another two years.

He left Merce with the impression that her sister was ill, and oblivious to my father's true intentions. So much so that she felt impressed by her brother-in-law's thoughtfulness and gladly accepted.

That night my mother called. She spoke with Merce and told her my father took her children without her permission and he took her vehicle keys and hid her vehicle, so she did not have any transportation, but she was going to take a bus to Riverside as soon as possible to pick up her kids. My aunt told her to take advantage of not having her children and get some much-needed rest. I'm not sure how their conversation transpired but before hanging up she asked to speak to my brother. She did not want to speak to me. She was upset with me because she felt I could have protested against going to Riverside without her permission and I didn't.

She didn't ask to speak with my sister either, she had a special bond with my brother... he was her boy. My sister was a daddy's girl and I was both. My father had taken my mother's vehicle to tía Soco's house. He told her the same story he told Merce and expressed concern about her driving to Riverside to pick up the children. She allowed him to store the vehicle in her backyard. The days transpired and I did not hear from my mother again. I don't know if she made any contact with Merce again, if she did, they kept it from me.

It was the early dawn hours of Wednesday, April 1st, when the telephone rang. I was awake because one of my cousins was getting ready for work. I heard her tell my aunt it was odd for such an early phone call, as she ran to answer the telephone. I didn't hear much and didn't know who she was talking to, but she walked into the room, looked at me and closed the door. Shortly after I heard tía Merce crying but I couldn't make out what she was saying.

Later that morning, I went grocery shopping with her and she informed me that my parents had been involved in a terrible car accident in San Diego. She said as a result of the accident, my mother was in the intensive care unit with major injuries and my father was okay and had been discharged. Merce told me she did not want to tell the twins because they were very young and would not understand. She wanted to wait to break the news to them. That story stood for about three days and how she thought a story like that would hold, I have no idea. All it did was confuse me.

Tía Merce and the others told me I couldn't visit my mother in the hospital because she was in intensive care and children weren't allowed in that wing of the hospital. I couldn't wait to see my Mom again and prayed for the day she would come home. I hoped and prayed, I was a child not knowing the truth, not having the slightest idea that my father was in jail and my mom was gone. That my father had killed her, and I would never see her, touch her or hear her voice ever again.

Merce was referred to a victims' advocate program that provided assistance for victims of domestic violence. In this case, they were providing counselors to deliver the news of the events that had really transpired between my parents. The counselors were coming over the evening of Saturday, April 4th. I knew there were some people coming over to speak with the *cuates* (twins), that was the impression I was under since I already knew of the crash my parents were in. For the next couple of days, I prayed. I prayed with all my being. I asked God to protect my mother and make her well soon. I made promises to God in exchange for her health. I was worried but filled with hope because my faith in God was great and because aunt Merce had told me my dad was okay so if he was okay, she would be too.

Saturday was a great day; my cousin Bertha celebrated her birthday. I was super excited because I bought her a gift – some beautiful earrings! In my opinion, they were the best gift, and she was going to love them. She better because I had spent a whopping $2.99! I bought them at market where I had gone grocery shopping with Merce a few days before. The day went by and I had not gotten any updates regarding my mother's progress. I remember asking Merce if anybody had called her with news and she said no, she hadn't heard any.

That evening, the counselors arrived who I was still thinking were going to speak to the twins. They walked in and joined *Merce* in a private conversation. After a few minutes, they came back to the living room where I waited with the twins and other family members. It was a man and a woman. They walked towards me, and both sat next to me. I thought, wait a minute why are they here with me? Aren't they here to see the twins? I immediately felt a wave of cold air run up and down my body, as if I was going to be hurt by them.

I glanced over at my tía for help, but I couldn't speak, the vast uneasiness was overwhelming, then they began to speak.

"We are here to speak to you about your parents," the woman began. "Your mom and dad got into a terrible argument and your father had put his hands around your mother's neck and he just couldn't let go."

I was confused and still thinking they were in a car accident.

"How did he do that while he was driving? I asked. "Is that how he lost control of the car?"

The woman looked at me, held up her hands simulating how my father wrapped his hands around my mother's neck and said, "No, there was no car accident. They were at home."

I was totally confused by then, "Okay, where are they now? Are they still mad?"

She responded, "No, unfortunately your mommy has passed away."

"No," I said, "They were in a car accident, right Tía?"

I looked at Merce and her eyes were filled with tears. I looked at my uncle Rafael and he put his head down. I couldn't think fast enough. I couldn't say anything. Then I blurted out, "No, that's not what happened. You're wrong. She's in the hospital, right tía, right?"

My cousin Jorge was translating for my aunt, so I looked at him for reassurance, but his eyes were watery, and he looked away. As I look back on this now, I wanted her to be wrong so bad. I wanted to tell her to leave because she was stupid. She did not know anything. Who was she anyway? Just a stranger talking shit! I wanted to hit her to make her disappear. I wanted to get up and go with my aunt Merce so she could tell me the lady misunderstood, but I couldn't move. I felt numb all over. All I managed to express were the words, "No, no please! please no!" I looked at tia and I asked her is it true? Did she die?" and she nodded her head yes, she was confirming what the lady was saying. My mother was dead.

And I asked, "And, my dad, where is he?"

The lady said, "He is in jail."

I can't describe the pain I felt as my heart broke and my life began to crumble beneath me.

The man had been talking with the twins and the lady had now turned to join him. I'm not sure the twins truly understood what was going on, but they began to cry. I think mostly out of fear from watching my reaction. They were only five years old, and their life had just been turned upside down. I had spent a lot of time in Riverside, and I loved my aunt Merce. I felt at home with her and my cousins, but the twins only knew my mom and they were babies. They still needed her nourishment.

As I write this, my heart breaks all over again for my siblings and for me. How unfair. My chest is pounding with anxiety, my stomach hurts, it hurts to breathe, and I feel scared. My head is throbbing. I am drained. I am remembering how hard I prayed for my mother to get well so she could transfer to a regular hospital room where I could see her. Yet the whole time I was praying, she was already dead. I know God has a greater plan and there's a method to the heart-breaking madness but my God it hurts, still! I am in physical pain right now.

I can only imagine that's how it felt that day just a lot scarier. To 10-year-old me and the twins, I want to hold you tight and say you are not alone, it's okay don't worry, don't fear, you really will be okay if you choose wisely, you will be successful and happy. I want to tell them I love them and hold them tight because it's going to be okay. I want to hold my aunt and tell her she's going to be okay too and its okay to love these children and nurture them, be their safe haven and protector. Love them for your sister. I feel sick. I am a hot mess right now. I feel very alone in a dark cold hole.

From that night forward I only wanted to be with Merce. I only found comfort in her. I slept with her. I spent all day with her. I was glued to her hip. That following Monday the two of us went to LA to meet with my aunts, Carmen and Soco. We met at my house. As I recall looking back now, there were no signs forbidding the entrance, but the property was locked. We walked around the property, and my aunts located a window that was slightly open. They gave me a boost and between the three they managed to lift me the rest of the way so I could jump in and unlock the door for them. I climbed in and found myself in my parents' bedroom. Immediately, I felt that wave of cold air go up and down my body again like I had felt the day they broke the bad news to me. I quickly ran out of the bedroom and unlocked the door for them to come in. The house was a mess as if it had been ransacked and there was a foul odor coming from the refrigerator.

Apparently, the refrigerator had been disconnected and the meat in the freezer had gone bad. My tía Carmen thought it would be a good idea to tidy up her sister's house. My tías Soco and Merce agreed with her and they proceeded to put stuff back in order. Although their intentions were good, and they didn't really do much, they had completely contaminated the crime scene. They made my mother's bed and years later I found out that is where the murder actually happened. They had no idea they were doing anything wrong, to this day they probably still don't know how much they may have affected the case by entering the crime scene and cleaning the area. They were oblivious and felt they were doing well by their little sister. That probably eased their pain for a moment.

THE BLUE CASKET

The days that followed were filled with what ifs and different speculations of how the events transpired. Murder became a part of the dialogue that drifted through the house. Most of it was kept from me, and for that I was grateful. Family began to arrive from out of town for the funeral. Other than my grandpa Ramon, my mother's father, most of them were strangers to me, including another one of my mother's sisters. Her name was Rosario and everyone called her *Chayo*. These folks flew in from Mexico and I didn't know my mother's side of the family who lived in Mexico, but true to our Mexican heritage, there was food everywhere. Not only from what my family was cooking, but it came in from the neighbors and friends as well. Enough to feed everyone. Most people gathered in Riverside at Merce's house, some in LA with Tía Soco.

The day before the service, we all gathered at the funeral home. While writing this, and thinking back to that day, just seeing my mother's casket from afar was the most horrendous experience of my young life. The details of it all lay so vividly in my memory, my heart breaks over and over. I wish I could forget that day, but unfortunately, I remember all the details. The vision of my mother laying in that light blue casket is with me daily. It was a flat blue, with blue paisley fabric, textured finish with gold accents. Mom wore a peach color satin dress with a thin dark flowery trim around the neckline and under the breast area. Lupe, El Paisano's girlfriend, had made this for her. Her fingernails were polished with a shade of beige with a hint of mauve which I hate and stay away from when I get my nails done. Her hair was curled in some sort of an updo, and her makeup was done, very heavy. She looked horrific; she did not look like my mom. Her hands were very swollen and bruised. Her neck displayed poorly concealed evidence of strangulation and scratches. There was a heavy scent of flowers. I don't know if the undertaker sprayed her body with cheap perfume or if it was the flower arrangements or a mix of both. Maybe nobody else noticed it but to me it was pungent.

That night, I received an abundance of unwelcome hugs. I did not want to be touched. I did not want to go near the casket, I did not want to look at my mother. My Godmother insisted that I see her because I may regret it if I did not see her one last time. She walked me up to the casket and I saw her very briefly, just a sweep, but that was enough for me to capture every detail and permanently imprint the image in my memory. I did not want to be there. I wanted to grab my aunt Mercedes and leave. The funeral home was crowded. There were hundreds of people there. My mother had a lot of friends, a lot of people mourned her loss. There were a few dramatic meltdowns, displays of grief if you will. I had my moments, but I didn't want to bring more attention to myself. People were already staring at me, and I didn't want to be a bigger spectacle than I already was. At one point, no longer able to maintain my composure, I went to the restroom where my cousin Terry was trying to console me.

"It's gonna be okay, your gonna be okay." I couldn't stop my tears. I remember thinking, you say it will be all right, but I knew it wouldn't. I don't have my mom; I don't have my dad. I don't have my home. We are broken. Everything is broken, shattered into tiny pieces. I no longer have my family, what about the twins? What am I going to do? Who do I belong to now? My inner dialog was amped. I was shocked and in disbelief, the whole experience was surreal. I couldn't believe that was my mom inside the blue casket.

Driving back to Riverside that night, we were all very quiet. It had been a day for sure. They were all talking about feeling really numb and emotionally wrung out from both physical and emotional exhaustion. For me, it was abandonment, that's what I felt, loss and abandonment. How was I ever going to take care of the twins and me, what kind of life lay before us? Looking back, I guess we could say I was numb.

As we walked in the door, Tía Merce looked at the clock. "It's midnight". The phone was ringing.

Merce reached for the phone, "Hello." She waited, kind of staring at the phone. "Hello? Who is this? Who is this?" Suddenly her face had a horrified look and she said "Avemaria puricima!"

Tía Merce looked at me, then my Tía Chayo, and then handed the phone to her.

"Hello! Hello!" my tia Chayo said. "Who is this?"

Then, she looked at Merce and said, "Ay Dios!" and the phone fell out of her hand.

I picked up the phone, "Hello?

The voice struggled to speak Sa-ah-ha-a-ri-t-t-a I finally made out she was saying my name and I said, "Yes, I am Sarita. Who is this?" The voice then struggled in the same manner to say I'm your mom. The voice repeated the same statement again before I reacted and gave the phone back to my Tía Merce and she hung up. Tears came to my eyes. I didn't know what to think. The voice was raspy, like the woman was choking and gasping for breath. I was struggling to understand her, but I knew it wasn't my mom's voice. I'll never forget that sound, not as long as I live.

We spoke about it a couple of times, and neither of us ever mentioned it again. So many times, I have wanted to bring it up to Merce now that so much time has passed, but whenever we are alone and I feel like I want to, the coldness moves up my body and I change my mind. Then, one day, not too long ago, I finally spoke to Merce about the phone call that night. She remembered it immediately. She said it was a horrific sound coming from the other line. She said it felt malevolent, like something sinister. Unlike me, she did not understand exactly what was being said by the voice and she could not recognize the voice, but she felt it in her core and she feared it. She said it did sound like someone suffocating and gasping for air. She felt goosebumps remembering the experience and she stated she felt the awful feeling all over again just thinking about it. Although she didn't hear the same thing I heard she knew whatever it was it was attempting to sound like my mother but she said she didn't think it was my mother because my mother died a martyr and thus had gone to heaven (totally Catholic) and whatever was in the other side of that receiver was evil.

We had to get up early and go back to LA the next morning for the mass and the committal. Some of my teachers, my school principal, of course the family, and Lupe, El Paisano's girlfriend, also made an appearance. We buried her in Monterrey Park, at Resurrection Cemetery alongside my great grandmother Hermila, my grandmother Lina. I don't visit because it's a vile reminder that she was taken from me and now I get to stare at a piece of lawn and pretend to believe she is in there, happy, I'm there to see her? No thanks. It adds insult to injury. My relationship with God is great.

I do have unending faith in God and follow most practices of the Roman Catholic Church, but I don't attend the Holy Mass every Sunday which will disqualify me from being considered a 'devout catholic'. I'm not worried about it and nobody else should be either.

When my time comes to rest in peace, I will be cremated. Although The Vatican has issued guidelines recommending, keyword here is *recommending: that the cremated remains of Roman Catholics be buried in cemeteries, rather than scattered or kept at home.* I will go home with my children. They can request to have my cremated remains divided into three different urns or they can pass me around periodically. I always did enjoy going out. My cousin Terry was right, things are okay, I am okay.

THORNS IN MY HEART

*S*till sitting on the patio, I glanced over at my phone. 4:00 p.m. I could just see my aunts and uncles all gathering and discussing bringing their brother home to his final resting place and placing him in his mother's crypt, which was something I had never heard of before. I got up and fixed myself some coffee. I had thought of taking a walk down to the water, but I didn't think there would be enough time.

I wrapped my hands around the hot cup of coffee. I found the air warm but invigorating. There is something about all of this, whether it is the energy generated by the peaceful sea or is it that my dad feels closer to me here. Sipping the coffee, I began to wonder how one family could take so much and still hold together. This was a question I had asked myself a lot lately.

I remembered back when the Novenario (Novena), where the Holy Rosary is prayed for nine consecutive days after a person dies, was done for Mom, and it was finally over, my ten-year-old self wanted nothing more than for everyone to go home. I have never struggled with voicing my opinion, and I am not usually one to tuck away my feelings. You'll know what kind of day I'm having because it is written all over my face.

Everyone was leaving, but there was still one cousin who was riding my last nerve. He was here from Mexico with his mom, aunt Chayo, my mom's second oldest sister who was a bit outspoken herself. I decided she was not going to be on the favorite aunts' list. I had met this cousin before when he would visit my mom. He would hug her and keep his arm around her as he talked to her and I did not like that, not one bit. I would physically remove his arm and tell him not to touch my mother. Now he was pulling the same *lovey dovey* moves on Merce and I was definitely not in the mood for him this time around.

I thought to myself, his mother is here, why doesn't he hug her? So, I told him, "Hey, your mother is standing right there. Why don't you hug her? Please don't hug my aunt."

He said, "My mom is your aunt too and Merce is my aunt too."

Before I could catch myself, words were flying out of my mouth. "Yes, but I don't like her. I don't even know her and the Novenario is over, and all the visitors are gone."

His mother turned to look at her sister and said, "Well Merce! Looks like it's time for us to leave. It sounds like your little girl doesn't want us here anymore!"

Merce was mortified. She gave me the *you're in trouble* look and immediately attempted to do some damage control.

"You know she is still very young, and she has just lost her mother." In other words, please excuse her she's a little crazy right now.

They left shortly after. That cousin would visit occasionally, and I was always glad to see him leave. As I got older, I learned to appreciate him and started liking him very much.

.ୱ୭.

Though I had spent time in Riverside and went to school there, this time it was a different experience. I was coming from East Los Angeles where 99% of the children in school were Latino. I wasn't really exposed to other races on a regular basis. Where I came from, girls my age did not wear makeup or have boyfriends. I was now in a classroom with White and Black kids. Some of the little White girls in my 5th grade class wore makeup and had boyfriends who they would hold hands with during recess. Of course, those liberties would not apply to me. My family was very conservative and traditional. I would have to wait till at least 17 years old to attempt those shenanigans.

I was back riding the school bus as well. This time the bus stop was no longer across the street. The school district had moved the bus stop and added a few more stops to the bus route. These changes were made after the car hit me, in an effort to prevent children from crossing a street when catching the school bus. I learned this when I overheard the bus driver talking about transportation services making a safer bus route after a little girl was hit by a car on Valley Way and 36th Street a few years ago. I said, "Hey that was me!" It was the same bus driver. She said I nearly gave her a heart attack as she helplessly witnessed the accident. It was nice to hear that the district had taken notice and did something to make it better for the other kids. Even when it's bad, it's good!

I couldn't wait to tell Rosarita Refried Beans about how different it was here. Rosarita Refried was the one person I would share my secrets with, well one of her sisters, my cousin Nancy, was also topping the chart on my VIP list. They were both older than me, but they were the best. I remember telling Nancy that if mom ever died, I wanted her to be my mom. She probably thought this little girl is nuts, but she accepted, and I was thrilled. Little did I know the position was just a few months away from becoming available.

My life was turned upside down. No more walking to the liquor store for saladitos (**salted plums**). No more playing in the street or Fresno Park adventures, no more Rosarita Refried Beans and most unfortunate, no more Mom and Dad.

Aunt Merce had six children, four boys and two girls. The two oldest were females, one was married and out of the house. The two older boys were away in the military. The third boy was already 18 and a senior in high school. She only had one young boy at home, and he was in the 10th grade. Merce was and has always been a homemaker and my uncle worked in the dairies. Life in Riverside was completely different, very structured. We always ate together at the table, said grace before eating, we prayed the Holy Rosary at night, on Thursdays we went to the youth group at church, and we went to mass on Sunday.

I was not used to that lifestyle; I had been running amuck. Merce was sleeping with me at night for a few weeks but I'm sure she wanted to go to her normal life of sleeping in her bedroom on her own bed. Eventually, she did. I cried every single night for a very long time. I would be good during the day. I felt okay. I was adjusting to change but at nightfall, everything would go downhill for me. I would try not to cry because it would bother my cousin. She would say what do you want? Now, why are you crying? Stop crying! I wasn't trying to bother her or make noise; I couldn't control it. I wanted my mom. I wanted my parents. I wanted LA.

The twins were really in for a change. They were only five years old and did as they pleased at home with our parents. Mom constantly babied them, as she should because they were her babies. Their life was affected a lot more than mine. I had spent a lot more quality time with my parents. I have a lot of great memories. Unfortunately, they probably don't.

Here, they were cared for, clothed and fed, but they were also mistreated. Terribly mistreated. I am grateful that Merce took me in and kept me out of the foster system. She did the best she could with what she was handed. She had already raised six children and now she had three more that she did not ask for, and certainly not under the circumstances. She was mourning the loss of her little sister and now was going to raise the three kids her sister left behind. She did not have to, but she did it to the best of her ability. My little sister is the spitting image of my father thus, a constant reminder of him to Merce. You look like your father is something that she would often yell at my sister when she would physically discipline her. There was one instance when my cousin knocked my little brother over the head with her knuckles.

It sounded so loud I thought, "Damn! That must have hurt." I hit myself over the head in the same manner to see how it felt.

She saw me, walked up to me and said, "you want to know how it feels? This is how it feels," and hit me the same way she had hit him.

"Oh man, yup! No doubt it hurt all right."

It's kinda funny now but it was not funny back then. It would be a whole lot funnier if she tried that shit on me now. My brother was seven by then and I was twelve. She was probably 24ish. I'm not sure if it made her big and bad or, if she thought the physical punishment would fix whatever horrible thing he had done wrong. Perhaps her reactions to his actions were merely a display of ignorance. I don't really care how she felt or why she did it, it was uncalled for.

We were no angels, especially my little brother, he was a hand full. Now in his 30's he still is a *problem child* with the exception that he is responsible for his own actions now.

Back then, he was a little boy, a victim of his circumstances. To make it fair, I'll say he was a misbehaving kid, but his behavior did not warrant some of the punishments my cousin delivered and that's the bottom line. He was broken by the loss of his mother and all of the events that had transpired in his short life. He probably didn't know how else to manifest his anger or express himself. I was only five years older than them. I couldn't care for them. I felt helpless when I saw the twins being punished and I couldn't defend them, and I couldn't tell my parents because I didn't have any. They weren't even allowed to sit on the sofa. They had to sit in the corner on the floor. I was not mistreated. I was treated differently than the twins, but it hurt me to watch them suffer. It felt like thorns in my heart.

Following our mother's death, nobody held them or told them they were loved. They never felt that nurturing warmth ever again. God is a fair God, and he takes care of his children. It may not happen right away, but you better believe he will even out the score. In some way or another, at some point in time, what goes around will come around and someone else will be on the receiving end of the physical or emotional punishment. I absolutely believe in discipline and will provide my children a healthy serving of discipline if they need it. With that said, I have never taken a belt to a little boy's bottom, bruising from his lower back to the back of his knees because a bag with keepsakes that I brought back from Europe for my friends, came up missing so I assumed he threw it away, *ASSUMED*. I have never put a little boy's hand on a hot burner for whatever reason it was, I don't remember anymore but there is no good reason for doing that. We all make mistakes, mostly out of lack of experience. What's done is done, life goes on and people forget their actions. I would hope that we could look back, re-evaluate our actions, and recognize and own our mistakes. Those experiences would modulate my approach when dealing with the public in certain situations that I am exposed to in the Law Enforcement field. I have empathy, I feel sympathy when dealing with a child, a victim or anybody without a voice. Those experiences supplied edification and moral obligation. I will never humiliate or physically hurt a child and I will never blame and punish a child based on an assumption.

One of his teachers noticed the bruises on my brother's little body while at school and it was turned over to Child Protective Services. When the social worker visited our house, she checked the bedrooms, the refrigerator for food and asked questions in regard to the way my brother was being disciplined. Merce was beside herself. She said there wouldn't be any of that at her house, so instead of addressing the problem, she gave up custody of my brother and he was sent to foster care. My brother spent 3 months in foster care where they took good care of him. He was lucky to have been placed in a good foster home. He was taken to the dentist and when I finally saw him 3 months later, he had put on about 15 pounds and he looked better. Eventually my uncle Salvador, one of my mother's older brothers, decided he would take my brother in and a few years later, my sister was sent to live with an older cousin in Long Beach. I could not wait until I was old enough to move them both in with me. I wanted to provide a loving home for them.

CHAPTER 8

HE WAS ACQUITTED

Not much time left, I went to shower and change. My aunt Dora helped me arrange the mass ahead of time and I had no idea what it would consist of, but I wanted to be prepared and I wanted to arrive early. I slipped into a black minidress with black tights and some brown knee-high boots. Maybe not totally traditional, but it was black. We are a family whose DNA is tradition and if one dares to vary any, beware of the road you tread. I had a purple dress with me, as well. Maybe that will work for tomorrow morning. And, then again, maybe not.

I dialed my brother's room. I could tell I woke him. He said he was just getting in the shower, and he would be ready to go before 5:00 p.m.

The sun was dropping lower on the horizon now, sending gold and silver slivers of light across the water. I could have stayed there on the patio forever, just thinking and sorting through life's challenges. Finally, I went down to the lobby to meet my brother and head out for this next page of our lives to unfold.

"You have the urn, right Sara?" my brother said. My brother and sister never called me Sarita they always called me Sara.

"Of course," as if I would forget the reason we were there.

I drove as my brother checked out the directions to the church. We figured tía Sara would know, but just in case. We drove into the driveway early, wondering if they needed something, but they were ready. Right off, I noticed no lace head coverings for these ladies. We got out and opened the car doors for them.

"You both look so nice," I said as they walked towards us.

"You both do too," Tía Sara responded in Spanish. "We've waited a long time for this. This will give us closure. All of us," she added with a heavy emphasis while looking straight at me.

We were in Guaymas Centro, and finding the church was easy. I was stunned. It was so simple, yet so beautiful. This was something my Dad had not shown me when we were here before. All I could do was stare at the massive church in the town square. The late afternoon sun setting the soft white building aglow. The main parking lot was mostly empty, just a car or two towards the back. We rolled down the windows and just sat there trying to carry on a conversation, waiting for the others to start arriving. It was hot, but I loved the feel of the sea breeze. When it was close to time, and we could see the others pulling in, we got out, a few more hugs from the others, and we walked up to the church. My brother opened the door for us, and as I stepped inside, the beauty felt shallow. How can these buildings be so hollow feeling I wondered. I was disappointed.

I counted fifteen of us. Mostly our aunts and uncles, and many of my cousins and my brother and myself, all here for a purpose.

For a funeral, it seemed very dry. The mass, lasting about forty minutes, was filled with the normal prayers, but none of us spoke. The priest "blessed his ashes" as we were not going to have a priest at the cemetery the next morning. We all bowed our heads one last time as the priest gave us a blessing *"In the name of the father, the son, and the holy spirit, you may now go in peace"* and we all turned to walk away. I carried my dad's ashes out of the church for the last time. We took our aunts back to the house, and then my brother and I met our cousins at the beach, to walk along the shore and talk. Somehow, I expected the mass to be warmer, being in Spanish and being with family, but we stood separate as we had always been.

It was about 11:00 pm before we got back to the hotel. I really wanted to spend the time trying to have a conversation with my brother. I could feel he had something to say, and it was making him very tense. But we had been at odds for some time, and we were with cousins. I am sure he was happy to have the cousins along, so it never got any deeper than just taking pictures and chitchatting. I knew he had broken up with his fiancé and that was eating on him as well plus he was closer to our dad than any of us, and his feelings of loss were obvious. He was feeling more alone and sadder than I was at this point.

I tossed and turned all night. I thought it would have been the best night's sleep ever, getting the mass over and just one thing left to do. Bury the ashes with my dad's mother. But I was awake awake awake. My whole life seemed to be parading before me on this trip.

Dad had been acquitted of our mother's murder. How did this happen? This was hard to understand, but it is what happened. He claimed self-defense and he was released in December of 1987. And then the custody battles started. He was determined to regain custody of the three of us, but Merce had already gotten legal custody of us and a restraining order against him.

The first time, the first of many, that we went to court, it had been almost two years since I had seen him. Although I missed him,

I was very nervous. I was appalled. I did not want to see him; I was not ready to see him. He was responsible for my mother's death. Even before we walked into the court, I felt a knot in my stomach. Tía Merce was just as nervous as I was after all she was going to see her sister's murderer now. As an adult, I can't even imagine how she felt. That feeling was hers alone. I'm sure she had a similar feeling of disgust. My stomach got more knots. I wanted to throw up. My chest was filled with bad anxiety. That feeling you get when you are on a rollercoaster, you are afraid of heights, and you know here comes the big drop.

Oh God, how I did not want to see him. I didn't realize it was him when I did. He had lost a lot of weight in jail. My dad always had a belly, but now his belly was gone. When I finally realized it was him, I had been looking right at him for a few seconds. He was smiling at me, he looked very pleased to see me in the few seconds we locked eyes I could see he was impressed. He was wearing a beige shirt and brown pants with brown shoes, and he had on his glasses. As a parent, I can't imagine how awful it must be to have your children taken from you and not be allowed to say hello to them or touch them. As it turns out, he killed his wife to prevent her from divorcing and taking his children or any of his properties. He thought as the father of his children, the judge would grant him custody, that's how it works but God had other plans. To get to the children's waiting room, we had to pass by a long hallway with chairs all along the wall. The hallway must have been about five feet wide, not very roomy especially with the chairs where folks sat to wait for their case to be called. Walking by there was dreadful, my father was sitting there with his sister Mary who had become his support system. I was afraid he would touch me, touch me with the hands he used to kill my mom. There was about a foot and a half between us as I walked by, not even watching where I was walking because I was facing the wall the whole time, it was very unpleasant. I must have been so obviously uncomfortable because the Sheriff's deputy came and took my siblings and me to the children's room. He gave me some water and told me everything is okay, this water had special powers and it makes people feel better. He was trying to make me feel at ease.

Our father didn't give up like I imagine many would have, but he went to court every year attempting to gain custody, but he never did. I was 15 years old the last time I went to court. This time, the judge addressed him and said:

"Mr. Paredes, you got away with murder Sir, but if I have anything to do with it, you will never see your children again."

That judge granted Merce a three-year restraining order, good until I turned 18.

The years transpired. I would jump at any opportunity to visit Rosarita Refried Beans and Nancy, but I didn't miss LA as much as I once did. Eventually, Rosa Refried Beans went away to college, and I stopped going to LA. I had become accustomed to Riverside. East LA did not seem as attractive as before without Rosa. My little brother was living in south central LA with one of my uncles and my little sister was in Long Beach with one of my cousins. I was not as sad anymore, only at certain times of the year I would feel a bit more listless. Every year towards the end of March, I begin to feel a bit sluggish and my heart feels a little heavy. I think it's the anticipation of the anniversary date of the worst day of my life that makes me feel blue.

I always felt incomplete, unsatisfied, I never really felt at home. Like broken and unable to find all the pieces to put me, us, back together again. I wanted to start my own life and bring my brother and sister to live with me. That was my goal from the time I lost my family. I didn't want us to be a burden to the family anymore. I really wanted to be an adult, finish school and take responsibility for the twins and make them feel more at home like they belonged.

It was 1994, and I was 17 years old. I had gone to LA for a family party. My cousin Roger was Soco's youngest son. Roger was four months younger than me, and he had always been shorter. He was like a brother to my little brother. He was my little brother's Rosarita Refried Beans. I had not seen him in a very long time.

When I saw him, he gave me a hug and told me, "I'm finally taller than you, Sara!"

That would be the last time I would get to see him. Unfortunately, Roger would lose his life a week later. His death was very hard on our whole family. He was the baby of his family, only 17 years old and had fallen victim to gang violence where he was collateral damage.

My cousin, Eduardo, was my tía Merce's oldest son. Eduardo was one of the pallbearers at my cousin Roger's funeral. After the mass, I rode with Eduardo to the cemetery. I was devastated and I couldn't stop crying he offered me a piece of gum, attempting to make me feel better. He was a humble kind-hearted man. I never imagined on that ride to the cemetery that only a month later, I would be mourning his death too. Roger died in April and Eduardo died in May. Eduardo was a cowboy. He would ride his horse every morning before work. On May 6th, he left for his morning ride, never to return again. There was an accident, and both he and his horse died. He was 26 years old. I was inconsolable, once again my heart was broken. I loved Eduardo very much. He was like a brother to me. Everybody loved that man. He was an awesome guy. There are certain people born with an indescribable quality. These people are unselfish, humble, considerate, modest and always a pleasure. My cousin, Eduardo, was born with that quality.

Now, in all of my 46 years, I have only met a handful of folks with that special quality. My uncle Rafael, Eduardo's father, who raised me, my cousins Rosarita Refried Beans, Lupe and Felipito, and my dear friend Ada Benitez, were all born with that special quality. They are truly exemplary human beings. Even if I don't see them on a regular basis, I love them and know I can count on them.

CHAPTER 9

IT WAS MY FAVORITE NAME

1994 was a tough year, filled with both sadness and joy. I lost two very special persons in my life, but I also graduated from high school that year and met a young man who would later turn out to be my husband and the father of my children.

I had very strict rules, which I often broke, but none the less they were implemented. I was not allowed to go out, but I was so devastated when my cousin Roger died, I think tía Merce felt bad for me. A friend of mine had invited me to go dancing, her parents were taking us, and my aunt let me go. She saw it as a form of distraction from my sadness.

The club was filled with activity when we arrived. We spent a few minutes surveying the situation, then we sat down in front of a group of boys. I did the twist and turn move to adjust my back and got a better look at our neighbors. Not too bad, so I told my friend to adjust her back and we agreed we sat in a good spot. I thought, Jesus please let the guy in the middle with the blue shirt ask me to dance and I hope he knows how to dance. Jesus came through!

Next thing I know there he was with his hand out and a smile. I said nonchalantly, "Sure." I didn't play hard to get this time. I felt an instant connection with him. He was a good dancer, but he didn't say much, he would just smile.

He did ask me my name and I told him, but I didn't get his. He was not very aggressive, compared to the other guys in the club, he was very shy. He was there with a group of friends and his brothers. One of the guys in his entourage went to school with me so he used that to spark up a conversation. I danced with another guy that was a lot better looking and older but was immediately turned off by his arrogance. I was hoping to get another dance with the shy, quiet dude. The older guy had come back and uninvitingly planted himself at our table. He wouldn't go away. I was very annoyed and simply answered yes and no to his questions. My rejection couldn't be more obvious, but he didn't care. I finally told him you should go with your friends; you're giving out the wrong impression by sitting here. He said okay I'll leave if you give me your number. I gave him a number. I don't know whose number it was, but he got a number. By this time, it was time to go home, and I never did get more time with the shy guy like I had hoped. The older guy decided he was going to walk me out, oh my goodness he was shameless and very determined. I got up to go but I made sure I made eye contact with the shy guy as I got out of my chair. He raised his drink at me as he gave me a smile and a nod, and I didn't look away, so he got up and began to walk my way, but there was that other fool walking next to me like he was someone special and I saw him glance at him and sit back down.

I never thought I would see him again, and I was bummed. I wish I would have talked to him and asked him more questions, but I was pretty shy myself. I couldn't believe I didn't even get his name.

Luckily, one of his buddies was still in high school and he went to school with me, but I had never seen him. On Monday, his buddy was waiting for me outside one of my classes. He said he had a class across the way, and he would always see me after class. He told me he had a message for me.

Immediately I got excited because I knew who it was from. In the most nonchalant manner, I said, "A message for me? Well, let's hear it."

He proceeded to tell me that his friend Joaquin said hello and wanted my number.

I thought Bingo! But I said, "Joaquin? Who's that?" I knew exactly who it was.

He said, "The guy you danced with on Friday."

"Oh, which one?"

He said, "the one with the blue shirt."

I had a favorite name which I had decided I was going to name my first-born son. I had even discussed it with Merce. Joaquin was the name of a good friend of my cousin Eduardo, and I thought he was dreamy, and I really liked his name. I would admire him from behind the window in the kitchen, but he had no clue I existed, I was just a kid. Tía Merce would tell me to get out of there; you're going to get caught staring.

"Tía, if I ever have a son, I am naming him Joaquin."

With that said, I was overjoyed when I learned his name was Joaquin, my favorite name for a male! In my 17-year-old little brain, I saw that as a sign from God and I should definitely meet this boy. He was obviously heaven-sent for me! So, I told his friend, "Well, tell him I said hello. That I dig his name and that if he wants my number, he can ask me for it himself." Eventually, I gave him my number and he called. We met two weeks after my cousin Roger died and two weeks before my cousin Eduardo died. I remember telling Eduardo I had met a new guy. I'm sure Eduardo didn't care much about my romantic endeavors but that night he pretended to listen and that was good enough for me.

Joaquin came at the right time, a time I needed him.

CHAPTER 10

THE BENEFIT
OF THE DOUBT

Dawn was just breaking. I pulled back the curtains and opened the sliding door, fixed me a cup of coffee, dropped the creamers and Splendas in, and went out on the patio. I just sat there in my pajamas, wondering about life. The fresh breeze blowing against my face had a familiar chill. I remembered mi papi telling me how cold the desert can get, even though the heat builds during the daytime, the nighttime can be extremely cold, and it is always coldest just before dawn.

A walk is what I needed. I hurried and dressed and slipped out into the early morning light. I had thought of going to the church, to just sit in its splendor and pray, but I decided just to wander down the beach and just think. My thoughts drifted back to when I was younger.

Joaquin and I dated for almost three years. He proposed three times. The 3rd time he added if you don't want to marry me then why are you with me? I did want to marry him. I was deeply in love with him and only he made me feel happy. I just didn't feel ready yet. I was too young, but I figured he was right, so I said yes.

He was not the typical 19-year-old. He was sweet, hardworking, very respectful and responsible. He had moved out and had his own apartment. I was only happy when I was with him, and I couldn't imagine my life without him. I wasn't interested in the other guys, and I had lots of male friends, but I only had eyes for him. He had my heart. As parents we want only the best for our children, Merce wasn't a fan of Joaquin. She warned me that I would not be happy because we were very different. He was born and raised in Mexico, and I was not. I didn't see and I did not want to see her perception.

She told me, "You don't see it now but mark my words, you will one day."

I was not interested in anything she had to say. My mind was made up and I was loyal to my love. I had a really good relationship with Merce pre-Joaquin. Eventually, we recovered our relationship. Today, I still talk to her about mostly everything pertaining to me with the exception of my romantic life. I don't keep it from her because I am a grown woman, but I don't share anything she doesn't ask about. I don't think she is necessarily fond of the stuff I tell her sometimes and some of my decisions probably shock her, but she listens and gives me her opinion. I hear her advice, and although I don't usually follow it, I always want to know what she thinks. I know she'll pray for me either way and that works.

There was Joaquin, and then there was my dad. When I was 18, I decided to look for him. I found him, but I didn't tell anybody because nobody was going to understand my reasons. I only told Joaquin and he took me to meet him.

When I saw him, it felt normal. I was no longer scared. I didn't feel like I did when I saw him in court eight years before.

I maintained communication with him, and I felt good about it, but he always had to make some kind of undue comment. I did not ask him any questions about 1987, I only wanted to see him again. I wanted a relationship with my father, I gave him the benefit of the doubt.

He voluntarily told me his story and I listened. I wanted to believe him so bad. I wanted his story to be real but deep down inside I knew he was lying to me. He was persistent about his innocence, about how much he had suffered during his marriage, about how much my mother's family had hurt him by taking his children. He was relentlessly attempting to convince me of his innocence which I never questioned because I didn't want to hear his explanations. I simply wanted to have him in my life. His claims of innocence only exposed his culpability. He did not want me speaking to his sisters, Rosa and Mary. He suggested I stay away from both of them because they were busybodies. I only had good experiences with his sisters, and I enjoyed both of them very much. His allegations came across as manipulative and erroneous, my doubts and disillusion only grew. Little by little the ugly truth would begin to reveal itself. Ugly but nevertheless, the truth.

Joaquin and I were married January 18, 1997. Actually, legally married May 22, 1996, but the religious ceremony is the one that actually counts. I'm Catholic, remember? He was 20 and I was 19. We didn't have money for a honeymoon and we both had to work on Monday. We decided to go to the Mission Inn Hotel. It's the fanciest hotel in Riverside and we thought this was a fancy occasion. After our wedding party, we went to check in and they turned us away because we were under the age of 21. Disappointed we went home to our apartment.

CHAPTER 11

LACK OF LOVE

The smell of the sea permeated my thoughts bringing me back to the present. As I turned the corner, it was no longer the sea but fresh baked breads that caught my attention and seemed overly familiar as well. I was headed back to the hotel to clean up and get ready to go, but this pastry shop... . The smell reminded me of being with my Dad. It caught me for a moment. Was it the fragrance of fresh bread, or had my Dad and I stopped at this shop years ago when we were down here? Maybe it was the smell of the fresh baked goods that reminded me of some of our outings before the twins were born. I just absorbed the deliciousness of it all. Good memories, laced in with the others. I turned around, walked back and just stared inside for a moment, then continued on my way. It was busy but the people all seemed not to be in a rush. Life is good.

My brother was waiting for me in front of the hotel. His usual flannel shirt, jeans and boots and a cup of coffee in his hand. His hair was much lighter than our dad's had been.

"I was beginning to wonder about you," he said.

"Just couldn't sleep much and thought I would get out and take a walk before we leave for the cemetery."

"Are you uneasy about going to the cemetery?" He hit a pebble with the toe of his boot, and it scooted across into the grass. "Why couldn't you sleep?

"I don't know. It seems my brain is flooded with memories, no matter how hard I try to file them away. They are just there. I don't feel emotional, I just really can't say how I feel."

"I noticed you hardly had anything to say last night to the cousins." He waited, in hopes I would respond, but I just shrugged my shoulders. "This has been a long process, maybe it is starting to wear you down, you think?"

"Maybe, but I noticed you didn't talk much either."

"No, but I don't normally."

I thought back to last night, remembering how I just wandered along the beach behind them. My brother and I really had nothing left between us. And, his twin, if they had ever bonded, that bond no longer held them together. I knew in my heart it was the lack of love from the moment our mother was killed, and life dumped them into this abyss of no motherly love and a lot of emotional and physical abuse towards them both, and they are now the product of that very thing.

I wondered then how much my brother actually realized the effect all of this ugliness had had on his life. All of that hurt me so much, the twins not being loved and nurtured. And now, we were living with that lack of love. Oh, dear God.

CHAPTER 12

HIS VERSION

For years, I never really knew what had happened to my mother. I only knew the different versions of what my mother's family assumed happened and what the counselors said. I don't think any of them ever saw the actual police report. It appeared my Dad had a couple of versions of what happened. His story that the family heard was truly a bit Hollywood, but it was possible. I shudder remembering his version. There were two males in the neighborhood known as "Johnny" and "Negro." They were well-established as the local dirtbags. According to my father, my mother had gone to the police with information about some drug deals involving the two. Her cooperation with the police was not appreciated by these guys and they were out to get her.

He said, at some point during the day on March 31st, she had left the house. He began to worry when she hadn't returned by 8:00 p.m. He waited until 10:00 p.m. and then went to look for her, but when he went out the front door, there was a man there with a gun. He said he didn't know the man personally, but he did recognize that he was part of the entourage of the two thugs.

Then, according to him, he was taken to the rear of the house, where there is an ally. He stated there was a car parked in front of his and one behind his. He was marched over to where the trunk of his car stood open and saw his wife's lifeless body laying inside. He said it was dark and he couldn't see much detail. They told him not to speak. He was instructed to drive, to follow the car in front of him. He said the man with the gun rode in the back seat of the car with him and made sure he followed the instruction he was given. He said they took the I-5 South towards San Diego. He was instructed to exit on Genesee Avenue. Once they came to a stop, he was told to wait in the car. He said he sat in the car while they removed the body from the trunk of the vehicle and placed it on the side of the road. He was then instructed to stand outside his vehicle until he was sure someone had seen him, then he was to get back in the car and drive home to LA.

To this day, I try to avoid the part of the I-5 Freeway that has the Genesee Avenue ramp. Seeing that exit makes me sick to my stomach and I begin to visualize what my mother's lifeless body looked like on that cold off-ramp, on the road like she was noth-ing. I visualize him dragging her out of the trunk and dumping her on the road with all disregard and disrespect. I remember him tell-ing me when he gave me his version of events that the men pulled my mother out of the vehicle and they had urinated on the ground. I also remember reading in the police report, in the part of the report that describes the condition of the body, that the body was wet. I know he lied about the men peeing because there were no men and the police report didn't lie. I can't help but wonder if the wetness on her skin was his urine? It didn't specify what the liquid was because it was just the condition the body was in when it was found. Why would he even share that with me? Did this man uri-nate on my mother's body? What the fuck! This is the shit that will haunt me every now and then. I can get lost in a rabbit hole of darkness when I start thinking of all that. I feel my chest tightening just thinking about this. It is like a black hole in the middle of my chest that doesn't let me breathe. It's anxiety building up and I feel a bit wheezy. The thoughts are so dark and so many, there are so many details. It can make me crazy if I let it. That's why driving by that off ramp fucks me up but I recognize it and immediately begin my talk with God. I have to because I'm driving. I can't lose my shit with my children in the car or whoever else is lucky enough to be spending the day with me that day. I've become so good at hiding my crazy and maintaining my composure I can minimize the internal meltdown in seconds.

He said he did not kill my mother and that he never touched the body and had no part in her murder. He said he was told to blame himself and he was threatened with the death of his children. He said he was horrified of the consequences he would pay if he didn't do as they ordered. When he noticed a man looking at him on the side of the road, he then got in the car and started driving back home. He was stopped at the San Clemente Border Patrol checkpoint where he was arrested.

Although the grief counselors had a different story, I decided to believe him. Believing him meant my dad didn't kill my mom, believing him meant I could tell my siblings his story and help them feel better. Believing him would lift a tremendous weight off my shoulders. Believing him would not give me my mother back, but I would have my father again. My siblings would have part of their family back.

I shared his version with the twins and Joaquin. School, work, marriage, life went on. Joaquin wanted a baby, and I wanted a house. We made a deal; you buy me a house and I'll give you your baby. He bought me a house and I gave him a son, a boy named Joaquin.

I had made a promise to myself, almost a pact just between my ten-year-old self and who I was to become. Right after we were married, I brought my sister in to live with us, and not long after that, my brother came. But, as I look back now, it was too late to give them the sense of belonging and love they both needed so much.

My brother wasn't getting along with my husband, so he went to live in a home for young adults under the age of 21 without family. Unfortunately, he had begun to drink in his teen years and by the age of 19 he had a DUI under his belt.

CHAPTER 13

MY CONVERSATION
WITH MARY

I had never understood why my Dad didn't want me to speak to his sister Mary. But what he didn't know, nor did he care to understand was I don't judge people or situations based on my family or friends' opinions. I determine who I like or don't like and why. I decide who I share my time with based on the way they treat me and my children. I will respect the fact that two people that I love and respect don't like each other but I will maintain an independent relationship with both of them because they both have qualities that I appreciate and need in my life. With that said, I maintained a relationship with my father's sisters, against his will.

The story my father had given law enforcement was that my mother had attacked him with a knife, and he had to defend himself. As a result of the altercation between my parents, my mother lost her life. That was more or less the story my mother's family had given me along with the suggestion that the reason he got rid of her was that he only married her with the intent to become a legal resident of the United States, which he had accomplished thanks to her sponsorship the year before he killed her. My mother was a legal permanent resident of the United States, and my father only had a visa. I was told he did not want me to be born and he encouraged my mother to have an abortion because my birth would prolong his commitment and interfere with his agenda. Obviously, she didn't listen, as you are reading my words now.

I don't know that any of the stories I heard about my father were based on facts or assumptions as my family are habitual assumers. I didn't care enough to question him about any of it.

I absolutely understand where my mother's family was coming from, after all, they lost their youngest sibling in all of this. And I can appreciate any ill feelings toward my dad. I respect all of this. However, my father's family is not responsible for what my father did. I hold no resentment towards his family. I love those who I am closest to, and I value all of his family. This being said, I need to share with you my conversation with Mary.

Sometime after the wedding, I was on the phone with Mary when she said she needed to share something with me about my father. Mary was closest to my father when he was arrested. She helped him through the whole ordeal and to get back on his feet when he was released. She asked what exactly my father told me that occurred on the night of March 31st, 1987.

I told her the story he told me, and she said, "No, that story is false. He killed your mother and he had help."

My heart dropped. Once again there it was, the wave of cold air up and down my body as I braced myself for another hit.

She began by telling me that when he was first arrested, he was a humble man. She never imagined he was going to walk away a free man. She had thought he would get sentenced to at least ten years in prison. She encouraged him by telling him to take advantage of his time in prison and study something to become a better man for his children. She visited him often so that he wouldn't feel alone or depressed. My father would simply agree and thank her for her kind words. Her heart broke for her brother because he had lost his children and his wife and now was about to lose a great deal of his future behind bars. Aunt Mary told me she decided to tell me the truth because "she was not going to serve as a coverup for a murder." She said the minute he was released and the fact that he was a free man settled in, he turned into a different man. He revealed his macabre true colors, and they were dark.

Mary continued, "Your father told me the reason he killed your mother was that she wanted a divorce, and he did not want her to take anything from him or have custody of you three. I was appalled as I heard the words coming out of his mouth. I asked him to stop but it appeared as if he wanted to torment me as if he enjoyed it. He was proud of his fiendish actions; he bragged about spending two years assembling the perfect murder masterplan. I didn't know if everything he told me was true because I had such a hard time believing he was capable of such horrific measures." She took a breath, and then continued, "He said he did research and sat in on some murder trials, telling me there was a trial he watched with similar circumstances in which the suspect claimed self-defense and was sentenced to two years in prison. He said he used that trial as a blueprint to follow. He thought if he got sentenced to serve anything along the lines of two years, he would easily serve his time and move forward with his life. He actually made fun of the fact that he got away with murder and now he was going to work on getting his kids back."

My father had a great defense attorney, my mother had nothing. He had no previous crimes, an impeccable record in his favor and she had her Bipolar diagnosis against her.

Mary said, "He waited for my mother to fall asleep, then he attempted to strangle her. She woke up and began to ask what he was doing. She yelled so he turned the radio on attempting to drown out her voice.

She never imagined he was going to kill her, why else wouldn't she run out? He attacked her and she put up a fight, but she lost.

Mary continued. "He killed her in her room over the bed. He told me he was having an affair with a woman that lived with a friend of his, one of our neighbors, a woman named Lupe. This woman entered the house after he had already killed my mother and helped him by changing the sheets and placing a knife under the bed. While Lupe altered the crime scene to benefit my father, he and two of his buddies, a man who he referred to as Negro and another guy whose name she couldn't remember helped him carry the body out the back door into the trunk of his car. His car had already been parked there by the guy whose name she couldn't remember."

I had chills up and down my body because I knew exactly who she was referring to. She was talking about Lupe, El Paisano's girl-friend! That fuckin' piece of shit shameless bitch. She was at my mother's funeral. She made the dress my mother wore in her casket! I just about fell out of my chair when Mary told me that. The other two turds were Johnny and Negro. There was no way she was making this up. She wouldn't know these people; she wouldn't know details unless my father gave them to her. She lived in San Diego, and we lived in East LA. She never visited us, and she didn't know our neighbors.

There was always the possibility that he lied to her for some ludicrous reason but why would he lie to his sister? Why would she lie to me? It just didn't make any sense. It had to be true. She gave me a lot of details, too long for this book and too accurate to be false. According to Mary, upon my father's release, Lupe left El Paisa and joined my father in San Diego. I remember hearing that she had left Paisano without warning and he assumed she had moved back to her hometown. But, instead, she moved in with my dad, but only for a few months, then she disappeared.

Mary was not fond of Lupe because she knew she was an accessory in my mother's murder, so she never asked where she disappeared to when she left my Dad.

I was aghast trying to process the horrific information. I had just learned my father was a sociopath. Only a sociopath would be capable of his behavior. I had granted my father the benefit of the doubt. I allowed him to be a part of my life, although deep down inside I knew my dad had killed my mom, but I never imagined it was a cold-blooded, premeditated murder. I thought he really did act in self-defense. But even that was hard to believe considering my father was a trained boxer and my mother a female and smaller than him. I don't condone any form of domestic violence, but if he was only fighting back, did he really have to kill her? Why kill her? One good punch would have incapacitated or disoriented her long enough for him to run for help.

Twenty years in Law Enforcement have exposed me to many versions of bipolar. Bipolar in all its glory in the back seat of my unit, as I provide a one-way trip to Mental Health. I never experienced my mother having an episode as severe as the ones I've encountered at work. Nevertheless, I understand the emotional burden that living with a person diagnosed with Bipolar Disorder may become. I understand enduring Bipolar episodes may become intolerable. As bad as it may be, it's not an excuse to commit murder. Walk away, get a divorce, remove yourself from the unbearable situation. Mary was not very popular amongst some of our family members, but I appreciated her because she was good to me. I didn't see her as often as I should have. When my husband and I were married we were very young, and she was there for us. She took the time to visit us and helped us when we purchased our home. I don't know why Mary decided to come forth to me about my father's horrific actions, but I thank her. I thank her for putting her integrity above her brother's best interests and I thank her for doing my momma some justice.

CHAPTER 14

HIS GUILTY FEELING

The cemetery was located in the hills above the water. I had never seen a cemetery like this before, but the rest of the family, all my aunts and cousins seemed to think it normal. There was no grass, most of the bodies were buried above ground it seemed and their caskets were encased in cement. Gustavo, the grave digger, met us there right at 10:00 a.m. and he proceeded to chip away at the cement protecting my grandmother's casket. Nana Chepa, my grandmother, her real name was Josefa, who my sister was named after, died back in 1990 of pneumonia. We were disturbing her, but I kept telling myself, she would be happy to be welcoming her son back into her arms. I had met her when I traveled to Sonora with my dad and I would talk to her often on the phone, but I had never met my grandpa Manuel who died when I was about 2 years old. This whole cemetery thing was a strange situation.

No one said a thing. We just stood there and watched. When the guy had broken through the casing, he asked for the urn. I handed it to him – he placed it inside and began to seal it closed again. There wasn't even a prayer. I felt the urge to step forward, my voice breaking: "Our father who art in heaven," I began and the others chimed in. That was the extent of our service. Dad was now with his beloved mother.

Finished, we started talking among us. It was like a deep sigh of relief. It felt like from all of us, but I can only speak for myself. My brother and I were going to be staying another couple of days so we could spend more time with my dad's family. But, right now, everyone seemed to be grateful that it was over, and time to leave this cemetery. There was no reception planned but one of my older cousins, Narcisa aka Chicha, made a nice dinner for us the next day. My brother and I left the cemetery and headed for the beach.

I took a long walk on the beach alone, thinking, mulling over what Mary had shared with me so long ago. I remember I didn't share any of the information with anybody other than Rosarita Refried Beans. I didn't tell Joaquin. I couldn't share it; it was awful, and I felt embarrassed. I felt confused. It almost seemed unreal, but my gut told me it was all true and subsequently, I cut all contact with my father. This overwhelming feeling of his betrayal was overpowering. I felt disgusted by him. I would think about what he did and how he killed my mother with his hands and the thought of him touching me or hugging one of my children made me sick to my stomach. I chose to block him out of my life but yet the moment I learned of his passing I felt a hole in my gut. I felt extremely lonely like I had nothing left of me or what made me. Both of my parents were dead, and I had no validation, like an unclaimed piece of property.

He didn't insist, he knew what he had done, and I think he sensed I knew the truth. Now I understood why he didn't want me talking to his sisters. It was his guilt. He was afraid of what they would tell me.

CHAPTER 15

DOUBLE JEOPARDY

I could see my brother aimlessly walking the beach, far to the south of where I was. The waves gently washed ashore, and I listened to the silence as the water rolled back out. Silence is magical. I watched, thinking of a conversation I had had with one of my coworkers when my father came up in the conversation.

"I don't have a relationship with my father," I said in a matter-of-fact tone.

"Why not?" he asked.

I gave him a brief version of events and he responded, "You actually believe that? What your aunt Mary told you?"

I stood there at a loss for words...then asked, "You don't?"

"Well, I don't know all the details like you, but I call it BS."

His name was Danny Garcia. Danny was a veteran officer and he reacted as such. "Have you ever read the actual report?" he asked.

Once again, I was dumbfounded, and at a loss for words.

"I'll take that as a no. Why?"

"I don't know, I never thought about it. I don't even have a file number."

"Find out what really happened, you need to know and now I want to know too," we laughed.

"Well," I said, "I have no time and like I said I don't even know the file number.

"Sara, if you don't have a file number, get one! You know what to do and how to do it and aren't you about to pop? There's your time girl."

I was now pregnant with my daughter, and I would be going on maternity leave soon. I am big on signs, and I took his opinion as a sign. As if God was telling me "Hey, here's your answers. I've lined them up for you, now go and get them." Danny made my day. I felt motivated and filled with intent. I went into labor two weeks later. Apparently, I wasn't meant for natural childbirth. I tried twice and ended up with three kids for a total of three C-sections.

I was home with my new baby, and I couldn't wait to get back on my feet and start my investigation. In most cases, a crime is investigated by the law enforcement agency holding jurisdiction over the location where the crime occurred. Since my mother was murdered in Boyle Heights, I contacted the Hollenbeck Division. They had no information for me. I made other phone calls but got no answers. Finally, I drove to their headquarters, to the records department and nothing. I was bummed out and exhausted. I wasn't doing this alone; I had the company of my two-year-old toddler who was not potty trained and my one-month-old infant who I was breastfeeding ... fun times.

I didn't share what I was doing with anybody, I didn't want to hear anybody's opinion or negative comments. It is the Scorpio in me. Keep things to myself. It is just a part of who I am. I had to make it home by 3 p.m. to start dinner before my husband got home from work. The next day I called San Diego Police Department. Bingo! they had information for me but would not release it over the phone. I had a mild meltdown and the lady on the phone took my information and told me someone would return my call. I figured I would never hear back, and I would have to drive down there with my two little relatives to handle it in person.

The next afternoon I got a call from a detective. He was a SDPD detective assigned to cold cases. He asked a lot of questions and asked me to give him a few days to do some research. I was excited! Finally someone was going to help me.

He called me two days later and asked for my address. He told me he had the report for me and wanted to deliver it in person to explain it to me and answer my questions. I was ecstatic! He drove to my house the following week and dropped the bomb on me. It was the facts, now everything Mary had told me made sense. Every anecdote in this book is long story short. A lot of details were left out or the book would be too long. This is as close to detail as I could get. If you have any questions or comments about anything in this book, I am very accessible, and you are more than welcome to contact me. He began by telling me that everything was in the report with exception of the autopsy photos. Immediately my stomach began to knot and the cold air up and down my back would not subside.

"Tell me your dad's version of events," he said.

And I did.

"He then whispered, "Unfortunately he lied. Your father did kill your mother. He claimed self-defense but he did it."

I began to read the witness statements.

Then I read the statements of the arresting officer. He stated my father was detained at the US Border Patrol checkpoint located in San Clemente. He said my father was cooperative and volunteered his responsibility for the murder. My father stated that she was his wife and he killed her because she attacked him with a knife.

Then I read statements from the next-door neighbors. The neighbors stated they heard the radio turn on around 11:30 p.m. They stated the music was loud and it went on for about a half hour then there was no more noise. After reading that statement from the neighbors, I turned into a different type of neighbor. I am that neighbor that will not hesitate to call 911 if I hear the music playing loud or any sounds of distress, I don't play, I will call. Not because I am nosey or I am a Karen. It is because maybe, if those neighbors would've called 911 that night when suddenly the music began to play loudly, my mother would still be alive today.

I read my father's statement, but by then I knew enough. He did kill our mom and he had help. Law Enforcement Investigator and Strangulation Expert Witness, Rachel Frost, states in her expert opinion that it takes 20 pounds of pressure to open a soda can and there's at least 100 pounds of pressure in an average male handshake. While applying the carotid restraint, if we apply pressure to the neck, just by flexing the muscles of our arms once we obtain the carotid hold, it only takes 15 to 30 seconds for a person to go unconscious. My father stated that he had a ligature wrapped around her neck 8 to 10 minutes because she would not stop resisting or let go of the knife. NO. That is a complete lie. It is not physically possible to deprive someone of oxygen for that long by cutting off their carotid. The victim would have passed out a long time earlier, which means he intentionally held the ligature around her neck long after she passed out. HE MEANT TO KILL HER.

After going through the report with me the Detective asked me if I had any questions. I said yes, I do. Why didn't he get any jail time for dumping her body? Why didn't anybody talk to me to confirm his statements and allegations involving me? Why would he make up a story for me if I didn't ask him what happened or for an explanation? Why did he get away with murder? He said they didn't speak to me because in 1987 children under the age of 15 were not interviewed by law enforcement which has since changed.

He said my father made up that lie because he did not want to lose me or my siblings. He said he couldn't tell me what went wrong or why he got away with murder, other than he had a defense attorney fighting on his behalf. He told me to keep in mind that this crime had occurred in 1987 and things were different back then. He said that if it happened in present time, the outcome would have been a lot different.

There were so many things I wanted to know. "Was there anything we could do about Lupe, Johnny and Negro? Would pressing charges against them for accessory to murder be an option?"

"Absolutely," he said. "I would be more than happy to assist but in order for me to open up a case against them, your aunt Mary would have to be willing to testify in court. I want you to really think of what could happen and would opening up that can of worms be worth it." He went on, "If they were found, placed under arrest and sentenced they may get up to 15 years in prison for accessory, meanwhile the mastermind behind the whole murder would remain a free man. Just keep in mind that this would be emotionally draining not only for you but for your siblings." Finally, he said, "He would really appreciate helping me bring my father to Justice if that was an option but unfortunately even if my father walked into his office and told him what he did, why he did it or that he simply did it because he was bored that night, he would not be able to act on it because my father had already been arrested and tried for that crime. A person cannot be prosecuted for the same offense twice as that would result in Double Jeopardy."

Because my father committed a crime in the heat of passion, he was charged with second degree manslaughter and then acquitted. I thanked the detective for driving to Riverside and sitting with me to discuss my mother's murder. I told him I would follow up with him after I contacted Aunt Mary to ask if she would be willing to testify in court against my father's accomplices. I wasn't surprised when she said she did not feel comfortable doing this. I definitely understood, but I felt I needed to try.

I was not mad. I really did understand her reasons. I felt at peace because I know that God was going to take care of delivering their justice. My father may have gotten away with murder thanks to the Double Jeopardy clause in the 5th Amendment to the Constitution. But did he really get away with it? He was never part of my children's lives, or my siblings' children's lives, they never called him grandpa they never met him. He didn't share any special holidays with us. He lived the rest of his life alone and when he died, he died alone in his car, on the side of the road. I would say living his lonely life was a well-deserved sentence. A sentence made possible by aunt Merce who faced him in court for years and our aunt Mary who chose not to stand by while her brother continued to lie. God is fair.

16

THE SIMPLICITY OF KINDNESS

One more day here and then we will be on our way home. I didn't want to think about home yet, and all that was facing me there.

I headed to the beach. Earlier I had agreed to meet my brother down at a restaurant on the water for lunch, but I needed some alone time to think, and he seemed more than happy to sleep in for a while. There was something magical about this water and the people here. They seemed so settled in their lives, so accepting as to the way things are.

I stopped to pick up a shell in the sand, and two teenagers, a boy and a girl, walked by. "Good morning, mam," the boy offered, and then the young girl said, "We hope you are having a wonderful day." The Spanish just rolling off their tongues. It's a friendly language, and it just feels right for me right now.

"I am, thank you! You two enjoy your day as well."

I watched them as they smiled, and then walked ahead of me and on down the beach.

Oh, oh, the simplicity of kindness. I thought back to my life. I had been two or three years younger than the two sweet souls who had just walked past me when our lives fell apart. They seemed so peaceful. I wondered what all I had missed out on. Actually, I have thought about this through the years, what would our lives have been like if our Dad had not taken our mother from us. But then I would shake the thought from my head, it wasn't like that. My life and the twins' lives took another turn in the road. Daydreams are just that, daydreams. Not reality. I was raised in reality, but oh how the daydreams would bring smiles to my face on those dark nights I lay in bed. What would it have been like, I wondered, to be raised down here on the water... and to call this place home?

As I walked, the water washing up on the shore, the color so dark and still a brilliant blue, I realize there truly is no living in the past. Our original path had been laid out for us, then that path was radically changed, and we were left floating, grasping for that tether to connect us to this Earth, to family that somehow we didn't feel that we quite belonged. Actually, to connect us to anything. We had to find our center again, our balance, and it was a rocky road, a few detours, but still to keep moving forward and create our own legacies for our children, that is what I knew we had to do. There were times I would dream of talking to Mom, explaining how terrible I felt about how the twins were treated, and that I would someday right this, when I was old enough. I felt she was still with me, just in another realm. I wanted to make her proud. I stood still, the water washing over my bare feet, my sandals in my hand, the sun sending streaks of silver through the water. I watched the water come up and cleanse the sand and go back out, over and over and over again.

That's what we need for our souls – to cleanse them of all the ugliness and learn to love and be loved again.

But, this life – this beach is not our story. Our father's story, yes, but not ours, still I feel closer to him here than I have in years. My one precious memory that I cling to was how at peace he was here when we visited his family years ago. He did know peace, now it is up to us to find our peace and regurgitating all these horrific memories of the past isn't the way forward. I know that now. I took another minute to feel his closeness – the happiness of his childhood. Tears clouding my vision, sand packing around my feet. It is time for me to move forward, to embrace my life I am living now and to keep trying to better myself with each day, with each breath. Everyone has issues in their past, we are not alone in this, but that is our past, and taking a deep breath and moving forward is the only answer.

I turned and started walking, heading down the beach to the restaurant where we had agreed to meet.

As I entered through the front door, I saw my brother sitting out on the patio that stretched out across the water. He had a beautiful table for us.

I was greeted by the head waiter – gave him my name and he guided me through the seating area to our table.

Huero was seated on the end, looking out over the water. I was a couple chairs down, thinking he might turn towards me. Back then, I wasn't the calm, centered self that I am working towards today. He was moody and arrogant, and I was not in the mood for any of it. "Ya know," I said, "it is too bad we can't sit here and enjoy this and each other's company. It's beautiful, the color of the water is beautiful. Mexico is beautiful."

I was the big sister who wasn't approving of much of anything in his life in those days. I could tell he was ready to talk, but this wasn't the place. I know he loves me and really wants my approval. Maybe it was that he had broken up with his girlfriend. I just didn't know.

"So, did you come up with any life-shattering thoughts while you were out walking?" I was a bit surprised that he was even interested enough to ask me.

"I did."

He pulled his eyes away from the water and looked across the table at me. At that moment, he reminded me so much of our father, even his eyes, although his were green and our dad's were brown, he had our dad's look. "When we are wrapped up in our past, we are smothering ourselves. We need to celebrate each day whatever comes our way. These are our lives, and we can make them into whatever we choose."

"No more past, ya mean?"

"Exactly. I know we have a way to go, but our Dad and Mom are both gone now. They can't change how things were for them, and we can't either, but we can take the good parts of what they gave us and move forward." I quit talking. I was afraid I would lose him.

"That's it?"

"Yes, what do you think of that idea?"

"It's an idea."

"Huero, I know we have had our disagreements, but I also know we love each other and want each other to find their place in this world and find some peace." I knew better, but then said, "I can feel you have something you want to talk to me about and I wish you would just spit it out so we can move on...."

He just looked at me with a vacant look, then took his gaze with Dad's eyes back out across the sea.

"Maybe tomorrow."

That meant enough, I knew it well and didn't dare go any further. "Maybe we ought to order before we lose interest all together."

"Yes, I think I will have a shot. You want some nachos to share, or shall we have this seafood dish?"

"Let's take the seafood platter. We can get nachos at home anytime."

CHAPTER 17

YOUNG AND NAIVE

I t was finally time to leave. We loaded up our few things and headed out towards Hermosillo to catch our flight home. We had told our family goodbye; they hugged us and thanked us and wished us well. Aunt Rosa had decided to stay a few more weeks with her sister.

I felt as if a ton of bricks had been lifted from my shoulders. As soon as we got to the airport with about 45 minutes to spare, Huero went to the bar. I was assuming for some decent conversation and maybe a shot or two, but me, I just sat down by the window watching the clouds pass by. I needed time to take some breaths.

It wasn't long before we boarded and were on our way. The plane wasn't quite as full as we had coming down, and it left a seat empty in our aisle. As we lifted up into the clouds, I felt a tinge of sadness, leaving Mexico and our story behind and hoping we had buried our Dad and all the horrors of our young childhood in that crypt. Maybe a new start for each of us.

My brother had been so quiet, appearing to be deep in thought. It wasn't his typical moodiness, but more accepting what is.

I kept waiting for him to start talking, he had said, "maybe tomorrow," well, this is tomorrow. It didn't take but a minute.

"Sara, I need to tell you something."

"Okay, I'm right here. I'm listening."

"I've been prospecting with the Mongols." His voice was low.

The shock sent waves of grief rolling through me. My heart felt as if it were going to break. He was staring straight ahead, not able to look at me. No wonder he picked the plane to disclose this. A place where I could not yell and scream and cry. Of all the things he could have been confessing, this was not where my thoughts were. My heart closed up like it was turning to stone. Fear and sadness ripping through me.

"Of all the things…. Why Huero? Why?" I sank down into my seat. Fear for his safety ripped at my inner soul. I looked over at him. He had turned and was staring across the aisle and out the window. This emptiness moved through me again. My dreams of giving them a home and showing them the love they never had had come too late.

I covered my eyes, whispering a silent prayer, "Keep him safe, dear Jesus, and let him see the light. Please hear my prayer."

"Huero, why are you doing this? If you aren't concerned about your own welfare, think of me and my children. It is going to ruin our relationship."

I turned away from him, so he couldn't see the tears that were welling up. It was all I could do not to break down and just bawl. My heart had fallen to the pit of my stomach, just as we hit an air pocket. I thought I was going to throw up. "You know that if you continue this nonsense and become a full patch member, you will no longer have access to my children or be allowed to spend quality time with them. You will no longer be welcomed in my home wearing your colors or any sort of Mongol paraphernalia bullshit."

Oh my God, dear Jesus. What have I done to deserve all of this? "Why not another motorcycle club, a good one? There are hundreds of clubs I mean if you have to belong to one why an outlaw motorcycle club?" The disappointment was overwhelming. All I could think is he's going to end up dead or in prison. What is the family going to think? Here we go again! Another fuck up by one of those kids. At this time, I was younger and had not done as much self-help and healing. I worried too much about what others would think. I don't know – maybe if I took a different approach about the situation my brother wouldn't have joined that fucking glorified gang because that's what it is, a branch of organized crime. I was angry but mostly hurt. Hurt because my brother chose his new-found brotherhood over my children and me. Those fuckers meant more to him than us.

"Sara, it is about brotherhood. Maybe you can't understand this, but the club is not what it once was. Maybe you should read a book about it and inform yourself what the Mongols are all about. I just wanted to tell you, and now I have nothing more to say."

"Fine. But do me a favor and place my children and I on a scale with your "brothers". If their importance in your life has more relevance and outweighs my children and me then go for it – do your thing, become a Mongol, but we are done."

Our conversation was over. When we landed, he went his way, and I went mine. I went home and life went on. I continued to cook, clean, care for the children, and work, wondering if this was the way the rest of my life would play out. It was that thing called life, working and raising my babies.

Hureo did his thing and became a Mongol. I felt disregarded and betrayed. It was a big *FUCK YOU* to me. He became the head of the chapter where we live. Then, he went to prison, and I see his twin sons every so often, but I don't ask about their dad.

I decided to put away the police report because I had the habit of picking it up and browsing through it every time I came across it. All that would do is ruin my day. I would get a stomach ache and lose sleep. I would immediately feel overcome by a dark depression. My chest would feel heavy almost like I'd struggle to take deep breaths. I had to put the dreaded report away. Out of sight out of mind. Plus, I didn't want the twins to come across it and read it. I didn't want to cause them any pain. They were under the impression that our father was also a victim of my mother's real murderers, that he had been forced to take the blame for his wife's death. I didn't want to break their hearts or cause them any more emotional damage. The only person I discussed the police report with was my cousin, Rosarita Refried Beans.

So, I hid it. I hid it so well, I couldn't find it when I was working on this. I called the San Diego PD and tried to get a copy, but was told because of the nature of the crime, they could not accommodate me. Right then I knew the guy that brought it to the house did this for me because I was in law enforcement as well. I can't remember his name, but I am so grateful that he helped me.

I had gotten legal custody of my siblings when they were 15 years old. They were now 19 years old. My brother had moved out of the house and my sister still lived with me. I had been married for 6 years. Although I had noticed a few indicators which led me to believe that what my aunt told me about "you don't see it now, but you will later." She had been referring to the differences between Joaquin and me. I was still very much in love with my husband. Early on, I had suffered another disappointment because my brother had gotten himself incarcerated. It was a very short sentence. He was out in no time but only to go out partying and violate his probation by getting a second DUI. He got himself locked up again. He had become fond of drinking, and it got him in trouble.

My sister had a few boyfriends by this time nothing serious or nothing anybody other than me knew about. She worked at the drive-in so she would get off work very late and I would have to pick her up. I would ask my husband to pick her up and he would say no, she is an adult she needs to figure it out or learn how to drive. I never suspected anything, I didn't see it coming, I couldn't believe it. I was very close with my little sister, and I had good communication with her. My husband had single brothers and cousins that would come over regularly. Very often my sister and I were the only females in a house full of young men. I told her that if anybody made her feel uncomfortable in any way, she could tell me and I would take care of it. I would repeat that to her, often to the point that I seemed to get on her nerves. As she would tell me, "Okay, Sara! My god you're always telling me that". My sister was young and naïve. I wanted her to know I was there for her, and I wouldn't allow anyone to hurt her or make her feel uncomfortable ever again. I wanted her to feel confident and protected, that's all.

My son would fall asleep with her often and the TV and radio would be left on. Me, being lazy, hated getting out of bed to turn off her radio and TV. I would ask my husband to do it. One night I woke up in the middle of the night and I noticed he was not in bed. I waited a couple minutes. I got up and checked the bathroom, I walked to the front of the house to check the formal living room, there was no light on, no noise, nothing. I went in to check the bedrooms which were located on the opposite side of the house from the master bedroom. Still no noise, then I heard something in my sister's room.

I walked in, turned on the light and there he was standing behind her door, in his underwear, trying to hide. Still, I didn't think anything bad was going on, I thought it was very odd but that was it. How stupid was I? Pendeja!

"What are you doing here? Why are you standing behind the door?" I asked.

He said with a smirk on his face, "Nothing, I just came to turn off the radio and the TV.

"Okay," I said, "So why are you hiding behind the door?"

He responded, "I don't know, I didn't want you to think bad."

I looked over at my sister and she appeared to be completely asleep. The next morning when I saw her, I said, "Hey last night, when I went into your bedroom, what was going on?"

"I don't know what you're talking about, I didn't know you were in my bedroom last night."

"Okay, well you know that if anything happens that you are uncomfortable with you need to tell me right away and I will take care of it."

"Oh my God Sara, you're always telling me that. I already know."

I was so blind, stupid, naïve myself that I didn't question either one of them after that, I never thought of it again. Six months later, my sister eloped with her boyfriend. This was a boyfriend I did not like because she was 19 and he was 28. About a month after she left, she decided to visit our tía Merce. Eloping was undoubtedly frowned upon, and she knew this. She decided to tell Merce the reason she had left with her boyfriend was that my husband was sexually harassing her.

Merce insisted she should tell me and my sister refused to tell me. She pleaded with Merce not to tell me any of that information she had shared with her. Merce did not tell me anything but she called my husband and sat him down to question him about my sister's statements. My husband came home and told me the allegations my sister was making.

Here we go again the cold chills down my back, the stomach knotting. I looked at him, "Is any of it true?"

"No, it's not true and you need to contact her and tell her to knock it off."

Before this happened she would contact me only at night time when her boyfriend was present and on speaker phone. He completely manipulated her, and she did everything he said. For almost a month, I attempted to contact her, and it was impossible. She was not answering. Then one day she finally answered.

She talked to me in a very nonchalant manner.

I asked her, "What you told our aunt Merce about my husband... is that true?"

First, she denied saying anything then she said, "Okay, nothing happened. He was just trying to seduce me."

"Why didn't you tell me this was going on? I would have never let him get away with it if he was doing anything against your will."

"I just didn't want to hurt you."

"So, you were just going to let me stay with this man who according to you is a sexual predator?" I said, "Come on man, he is 25 and you are 19 but I have a daughter you were going to let me raise my daughter and risk her safety with a sexual predator?"

What happened? I demanded There was silence on the other end of the phone. I said let me help you with this, "Did you have sex with him? Did you suck his dick? Did you guys make out? What exactly went on?"

She then began to tell me that she did not have sex with him, that he only tried to seduce her, but nothing ever happened between them. She said that he would always hit on her and that he would offer to pick her up from work and then go get a hotel room somewhere.

That did not make sense to me because on numerous occasions, I asked him to go pick her up and he never wanted to. I always picked her up from work. I said that is not true and I'll tell you why. That is not true because you work five minutes away and the minute that you guys didn't come home 25 minutes later, I would assume something had happened. I would probably start making phone calls to see if there was an accident or I would go drive around looking for you. Not because I thought there was something going on between the two of you but because I thought something bad like an accident had happened. I don't believe you for 1 second. Now if you want to make up a story about you staying home from school and him coming home early from work to be with you while I'm away at work, that I might believe. Her attitude took a bellicose turn and she said, "Well if you don't want to believe me that's your problem. I don't care, and remember when you walked into my room and he was standing behind the door in his underwear? Well that night he was in my bed trying to have sex with me and when I pushed him away and told him to stop, he told me to stop playing hard to get, because you know you want it!"

My heart dropped. I had completely forgotten that night and it felt like a bucket of ice water being dumped over my head in the winter. She had just reminded me. I was at a loss for words. I maintained my composure and simply said, "Okay, well if everything he attempted with you was against your will, then you need to file a police report."

My husband denied all allegations. I didn't sleep that night. Once again, the shit had hit the fan and splattered all over me. Because I lived within the jurisdiction where I was working, the station I was assigned to responded to all calls for service in my area. I went to work the next morning. I noticed people looking at me in a peculiar way, but I didn't imagine why. My Sergeant at the time pulled me aside and said, "Let's take a walk, I wanna talk to you."

I had a good relationship with him so that didn't seem odd.

He said, "You know, that call came in early this morning."
"What call?"
"The call you told your sister to make. She called about 0130 hours and the dispatcher completely put you on blast. She said your name, the station you work at, your spouse's name, your sister's name and the call types 243.4 PC sexual battery and 261PC rape. He said I'm letting you know because all of graveyard shift heard the call and it's gonna be going around the whole station. I want you to hold your head up because you have done nothing wrong. You know I got your back and I'm going to take care of you as much as I can. I already contacted that dispatcher's supervisor, and she will be dealt with because it was completely out of line and that should have been handled differently." He added, "I'm sorry that this is happening to you. You don't deserve this, and you are not alone. You will get through this."

I felt so stupid and disgusted. I was mortified. I wanted to run away and not face anyone. My heart was broken yet again by the people that most mattered in my life.

I tried my best not to break down, but I completely lost it. I was embarrassed, I was confused. Everybody at my work knew what was going on, my family knew what was going on. I was mortified. How did "nothing" happened – turn into rape, assault and battery? I did my best to carry myself with the most authentic nonchalant attitude I could generate.

A few days later my husband was interrogated and polygraphed. Due to the nature of the charges made against him, he had to leave the home. If he didn't leave the home, Child Protective Services would remove my children from my custody. Needless to say, he had to go. He went to Merce's house.

There was an issue with one of the questions during his polygraph. The question was whether or not there was any sexual penetration between him and my sister and that question was inconclusive.

My sister was brought in for questioning a second time because her story did not match up. That day she decided she no longer wanted to go through with this and dropped the charges. The investigator told me there was no doubt in his mind about my husband's innocence when it came to the rape allegations, but he said there was also no doubt in his mind that something did happen between them. "I don't know what happened and you probably will never know what happened because they both lie, but something happened. Maybe they were having an affair. Maybe they kissed. Maybe they were just starting a romance, but something happened between them, and they were both willing participants. He's innocent of the rape allegations but he is definitely guilty of something else. He admitted that he was turned on by her. He said they spent a lot of time alone while you were at work."

I never really had a real conversation about what happened with the investigator. I felt as if he was holding back detailed information that maybe he did not want to volunteer unless I asked. Perhaps he didn't want to make me feel worse. I didn't ask because I didn't want to know. I was absolutely disgusted with the few details that I did know. I was disgusted with this whole situation.

You need to leave him. If I had a dime for every time one of the investigators familiar with the case asked me are you still married? Or, why are you still married to him? They had nothing good to say about him. But they never really gave me a reason other than he was no good for me. Joaquin swore up and down, he swore on his mother's life he did nothing wrong. The lady is still alive and kicking but her son is a fucking liar.

"If you didn't do anything wrong," I asked, "then why did you tell them that you were attracted to her in your interrogation?

"They were pressuring me, so I told them what they wanted to hear because it was taking so long and I wanted to leave."

I gave him the benefit of the doubt and he came back home. All of this happened when I was 25 years old, naive, in love and oblivious. He was young too, but he took full advantage of that. Now in my 40s, I can't help but think how many times was I sleeping in my room while he was awake in my sister's room? What was I thinking? How did I not see what was going on right under my nose? God has perfect timing and maybe it wasn't time for me to move on. Maybe I needed to experience another form of heartbreak to gain the strength and courage that would give me the confidence to move on with my life when it came time for that.

CHAPTER 18

I FINALLY EXHALED

I settled in with life at home and work. A lot of things happened through the years, good times and bad times. Why I stayed with this man for so long, I will never know other than I thought it was what my family of sorts expected of me. Time passed and there were other questionable incidents involving Joaquin and relationships, drugs but obviously he was never guilty, he was always innocent. The evidence was always circumstantial. He's the type of man that I could walk in on having intercourse and he would push the woman off and say oh my God! what happened? I do not know what happened. I don't know who she is. I don't know where she came from. I don't know, I don't know. He would deny, deny, deny, and I would just give up. I didn't want to deal with the drama. I was just going through the motions, and he had been on borrowed time for a while now. I was no longer happy. I wanted out but nobody knew. I would tell him how I felt and I asked him to leave countless times but he never did and I was a coward, too worried about our families' opinions, mine and his and my children. I didn't want to separate their parents over my pettiness, that's how I felt at the time. I was so stupid!

I told him all I asked of him was honesty. I didn't care what he did as long as he was honest with me. I could forgive and overlook a fault because we're all human and we all make mistakes but a lie? No. That just adds insult to injury. I told him if I ever ask you a question that has to do with your extramarital activities, please believe that I already know the answer. I have done the research; I know how, where, when, and who. Please don't lie to me because I will lose trust in you. That was something that he could never understand.

The incident with my sister occurred six years into the marriage. Joaquin has a lot of type A personality traits. He is very hard-working, hygienic, impatient, controlling, demanding and punctual. He is a very formal person, the opposite of a jokester. They say that opposites attract, right? I often found myself in trouble on the drive home after a family party or social gathering. I would get a lecture for a comment I may have made that he felt was inappropriate, maybe too bold for his comfort. I'm not one to back down and I would stand up for myself, but it was very discouraging. I am well aware that I am "an acquired taste" but I hadn't just developed my personality. I've always been me. When would he learn that I was not going to change to accommodate his feelings?

As a child, I remember my mother warning me as we walked into parties and gatherings, to be on my best behavior and keep my comments to myself. I wasn't rude or at least I didn't intend to be rude. I simply spoke my mind and always gave my very honest opinion. I was a bit gall but there was no malice behind my words. I was just a child that thought out loud. I have an intense need to speak my mind and I have to deliver it before the world ends and I run out of time! My fellow Scorpios will understand.

All of a sudden, my personality did not fit him. I didn't pander his disapproval, but I didn't want to argue. I didn't want the drama, I simply gave in and moved on, but he was chipping away at my spirit. Little by little I began to separate myself from my family. I stopped going to family gatherings. First my family in L.A. then little by little my family in Riverside. My family in Riverside is my immediate family. That's where I was raised and that's who I would celebrate all of the major holidays with. He would put me between a rock and a hard place because I wanted to go with my family, but I felt that my place was with him. He was my husband, the father of my children. He wasn't just a boyfriend or somebody I was shacking up with. I had taken a vow to be with and support him and I did to the best of my ability. I began planning a mini vacation every year on Thanksgiving week so that we wouldn't be in town Thanksgiving Day and subsequently we wouldn't attend the family dinner.

He didn't like it when I had company either, especially if they had young children. Nobody really knew how much of a dick he really was. My husband appeared to be such a nice guy and everybody liked him. My family assumed I was the bad guy because he was so quiet, he was a quiet dick, but a dick nonetheless. I always encouraged him to spend time with his family and do things with his brothers, brotherly activities. Unfortunately, they didn't really include him in any of the family activities, except when his parents were in town. If his parents were in town, all of a sudden it became the most unified and perfect family ever. His phone would start ringing from early in the morning and it wouldn't stop until he arrived wherever the gathering was that day. When his parents were in town they would get together as a family every day. Their unity went from 0 to 100, the hypocrisy was unbelievable.

He was very hard-working and an awesome handyman; I will give him all the credit he deserves. He did everything outside of the house, I never had to worry about taking the trash out, the yard, washing my vehicle or fueling it. He took care of that. He helped with carpooling the children because they were involved in different sports and after-school curricular activities. That was a great help but it's also the basic duty of a father. He was an outstanding provider but there was absolutely no above and beyond. He worked and brought home a paycheck. He had no clue what it was like to grocery shop or maintain a home, everything was taken care of for him. I walked on eggshells to make sure that everything was always smooth sailing. I did what I had to do to maintain a smile on his face and avoid conflict. I couldn't speak freely with him. I had to censor everything. I couldn't discuss a problem with him, if something came up like a problem with a bill or our oldest might have done something wrong it would be completely blown out of proportion. He did not know how to handle a problem, so I made sure he didn't have to deal with anything unpleasant.

I never could quite figure out what his issue was with our oldest son, all I knew was I always found myself covering for him, because if he was late, or just about any other reason, my husband would just go off on him. I was always stressed because I didn't want to get lectured and couldn't stand to see him always at odds with his dad. Please understand I didn't have communication with him because we couldn't communicate, he does not know how to have an adult conversation. Absolutely any little thing throws him over the edge, and everything is negative. He never had anything nice or positive to say about me or our oldest. He had no idea what constructive criticism or words of affirmation were. He only ever had negative shit to say, from the time he walked in the door it was a constant nagging. I felt alone in his company. As I said, Joaquin was a good provider with an impeccable work ethic, but he was a poor partner and his parental skills are definitely questionable. I am far from perfect, but I put all my effort into it every day. I will never stop working on myself to be a better person and mother to my children, no matter their age.

I wasn't afraid of him; I just didn't want to deal with his negative attitude. He didn't yell much but he had this look of utter disgust and disappointment that made me feel disposable and unworthy. We were separated 10 years into the marriage, but he was always there. I couldn't get away from him. While we were separated, if I went somewhere he would show up wherever I went. He would use the kids as an excuse to be over at the house all the time. That year he was involved in an auto collision and sustained major injuries which resulted in him coming home upon his release from the hospital. It took about 8 months for him to be back on his feet and back to work.

I addressed the issue of our separation and asked when he was going to move out.

"I am not moving out because this is my home," he said. "If you don't want to be here with me, you can leave."

At the time, I was 28 years old and it seemed impossible to up and leave with my two little ones. We never fixed the issues, we couldn't because he never recognized that there were issues. I didn't want to fight; I didn't want to create an even greater awkward and unpleasant environment than the one we were already in. Once again I threw in the towel and life went on. The pressure to maintain a pristine home all while working 10-hour shifts was always present. I didn't have any days off, but I couldn't complain because if I did, he would tell me to quit my job – that way I wouldn't be tired. Dinner was always waiting for him. If I wasn't home, it was left on the stove for him to serve himself. I packed his lunch every morning, his clothes were always on point. He was styled and pressed.

He didn't appreciate it because it was the way he was brought up. I was expected to take care of his needs and put myself last. I was raised in a similar environment and since I was married so young, I thought I was doing the right thing. I thought that was normal. At work, it was normal procedure to change out of your uniform in the locker room and wear your civilian clothes home. I never changed out. I would throw on a sweater to cover up my agency patches and rush home full uniform boots and all. I had to arrive before my husband to avoid upsetting him and to have his dinner ready. I didn't want to give him a reason to complain and tell me why I needed to stay home and not work anymore.

There was one instance during my eighth month of pregnancy with my daughter, where he crossed the line. I had served him dinner then myself, he was always first. After eating my food, I picked up the table and finally sat down to take off my boots. At eight months pregnant, I was exhausted. I sat down, took my boots off, and he says to me "*¿ oye doña y esos platos quien los va a lavar??*" "Hey ma'am, who's going to wash those dishes?"

I said, "Really? That's what you're worried about right now? I'm exhausted. I want to take off my boots. I want to rest. I need to rest." Then I said, "You are something else and one day you're going to be alone in a big clean house because that is your priority."

He was not the type of father that came home and greeted his children or asked how their day was. He came home and the first thing out of his mouth was did you clean your room? I'm gonna go check.

There were certain assignments at work that required overtime or being on call. I was assigned to the traffic team which was an on call position at any given moment a fatality can occur and as a traffic officer, you are expected to answer your phone and respond to the scene for the investigation. If I was off duty and my sergeant called me my stomach turned into knots. I didn't want to answer because I knew it was a call out for a fatal collision and I would need to respond. It was my job, and I was getting paid, but he didn't care. There was always an issue with anything work-related outside of my regularly scheduled shift.

He didn't support anything that would require me to leave my home for anything else other than my job whether it be to finish my education or work more hours. I always managed to sneak things in. For example, I took a course to be professionally certified as a makeup artist, but I couldn't really practice it because it required me to spend time away from home and he was not having it. If I wanted to be me, there was a price to pay.

The awkward silence and bad attitude would disturb the peace at home. If he was having a bad day everybody was having a bad day and that was unfair for our children. I felt as if I had to shut myself down to let him be happy, so that he felt confident and in control. I was content I had everything I needed but I wasn't happy. The first time I left my husband, I remember two of my cousins telling me I was making a mistake. They said, "it's not like he beats you." I guess it's okay for your man to be a passive aggressive control freak and a liar as long as he doesn't beat the crap out of you. It's amazing how an educated woman can be intelligent yet be so ignorant and oblivious.

A lot of women live that way because what is the family going to say? Because I've been here so many years, I'm so old, why leave now? They are afraid of judgment. They don't think they're going to make it financially, They don't want to upset the children. But are they really happy? Others can't fully enjoy their life because they're so worried about what "they/the family" are going to think, they always want to keep everything hush-hush. News flash nobody cares about your life if they did, they would write you a check every month. Yes, they probably have an opinion because they're nosy and they have to have an opinion about everything, but their opinion doesn't matter...I say fuck it. FUCK IT. Live your life and live it to the fullest. Life is beautiful and it is way too short to be worried about what "they" are going to say.

Unless "they" are funding your existence like putting food on your table or paying your bills, "their" opinion is irrelevant. I made the mistake of caring what my family was going to think, and what my in-laws were going to think, and I was a coward.

As I stated earlier, for reasons that I will never know, my husband never got along with our firstborn. He always treated him differently. I always assumed it was a personality clash because my son is a jokester and his dad is not. The older my son got the worse their relationship became. I should have left then but I didn't because he was not an only child, I had two other kids that I thought needed their father. I felt I would be doing my children a disservice by leaving him, as I didn't think I would be able to provide them with the same level of comfort they were used to. I knew my husband was not going to move out and I would be forced to leave the home with my children. I didn't want to relocate my children to a different area and school.

Looking back now and making the decision of staying in my marriage for my children's sake is a decision that I will always regret. I knew the damage was done between my husband and me. There was no more room under the rug to sweep any more "small mistakes," no more room for any more of his as he called them "that's nothings". He was full of lies and excuses, he was on borrowed time and the clock was ticking. He was never going to take responsibility for his actions. I had given him the best years of my life and vice versa, we had done the marriage counseling thing which was his idea until it no longer worked for him when the counselor told him she couldn't help him if he was going to continue to lie to me in front of her.

I would like to take this moment to say – Although another man was not the reason I left, I did begin to disregard my marriage I completely checked out, and had no problem acting single. I think I wanted him to feel discouraged and disappointed and give up on me. I moved out of our room and into my daughter's room I avoided him at all costs because things had gotten really bad. It got to the point where I couldn't be home if he was home, definitely not home alone with him because he would force himself on me. He blamed my leaving him on another man. He still blames another man for breaking up his marriage. The ONLY man that ruined our marriage was him.

I have never had a problem expressing myself and voicing exactly what I need and what I want, and he was well aware of my feelings or lack thereof, but he had established himself in denial. I was no longer in love with him, and I had no respect or admiration left for him. I was no longer submissive, and I was no longer considering him or his feelings when I made decisions. I decided I was done. I didn't want to turn forty and be in the same unhealthy circumstances. I left, I took my two minors and I left. My oldest son stayed as that was where his friends were. He wanted me to stay and have his father leave, but I knew that wasn't happening. Joaquin tried to convince me to stay. He made all the promises he always made but it didn't work this time. I was done, I finally exhaled. My oldest son slowly migrated to my new home and moved in with us.

It's been hard, one of the toughest decisions of my life but I don't regret it. If your life isn't what you imagined, you have the power to change it. Make a decision, the first step to getting what you want is having the courage to get rid of what you don't want. We all have a story to share, ups and downs that lead us through different trials and tribulations. Today, I live with my two sons and my daughter, and we have our struggles because life is always a struggle, but we are at ease, in peace – no eggshells to walk on in our home. If there's a lesson and a blessing in disguise every time. Find the lessons and count your blessings.

MY PARTING THOUGHTS

*N*ow a couple of years have passed and as I look back on my life, I couldn't be happier as to where it has taken me.

I purchased my own home where my three children and I live happy and carefree. Little by little I've been healing but I am definitely a work in progress. I learned that by recognizing all that is great in my life, the not-so-great seems so insignificant.

I have had some really hard times as a single parent because I was so disgusted by my ex-husband when we divorced, I wanted nothing from him. I left with my two youngest children and our clothes. I declined alimony, a desicion based on pure emotional, irrational thinking. At the time it seemed like the right thing to do. I wanted to move on and start my new life. I wanted to do it without his help. I see now that was petty, prideful nonsense. I should have taken what I deserved after a 20-year marriage where I gave my all and my return on investment was not the best. I took the short end of the stick. I am where I want to be now; I get to live my best life and sharing all of that with my children is my reward. I let go of everything and everyone that was not a joyous asset in my life. My emotional intelligence was screaming at me to let go, let go or get dragged! One of my main objectives is to protect my peace of mind, my time and my personal networks. Maintaining healthy boundaries and making your expectations clear will establish the behavior you are willing to accept from people and vice versa, in all of your relationships.

This past year, I lost my Tío Rafael who raised me and showered me with love, a love beyond what he was asked to give. His passing was very painful. That man was unique and irreplaceable. Letting go of him was not easy, but he was suffering too much already. Deep down I knew he had given us all enough and it was time for him to go. I could see the pain and suffering on his face. The last three years of his life he were in and out of the hospital, he had so many close calls, but the time for him to meet his creator was yet to come.

The Catholic in me had me convinced that maybe there was something naughty he did as a young man and all this suffering was his penance. That he had to make amends with whatever was holding him back from rejoicing in heaven. Why else would he suffer so much? He didn't deserve it. He was such a hard worker and being married to my Tía Merce should have gotten him a golden ticket to the pearly gates! I believe he made it to his final destination. There is no doubt in my mind my mother was there to greet him and thank him for loving her children. I believe all his pain was worth his reward and in heaven he is saying… Even when it's bad it's good!

We all must remember, nobody will help you if you don't help yourself. There are free resources out there: books, podcasts, life coaches and therapists. Some of my favorite books are any of Mel Robbins or The Four Agreements by Don Miguel Ruiz is a must!!, *The Secret* by Rhonda Byrne was a great book, and The World Is Yours - The Awakening by Kurtis Lee Thomas. Straight up Sisters the podcast, is a great podcast that addresses all issues we come across in life for single and married women. They have amazing speakers and resources on that Podcast. Nicole Lapin wrote a great book called Rich Bitch that teaches great strategies for financial sucess. Anabell Ingleton is an outstanding trauma-informed life coach that has been through hell and back. Considering it takes a special person to understand special circumstances and although I do feel that any form of therapy is helpful, I strongly encourage anyone that has lived through a painful experience in their life to seek the help of a trauma-informed therapist or life coach. Sometimes it may be expensive, but we are worth it, YOU are worth it. If that is the case, ask for a payment plan, speak up about your financial burden. Remember, "a closed mouth **don't** get fed". Don't be afraid to ask and if they say no, chances are they will work with you to facilitate the payments for you.

Utilize me as a resource, shoot me an email, I can point you in the right direction. Start each and every day with gratitude. However small you feel or what little you think you have there's always someone less fortunate than you. When you feel that warm water in your shower, those warm blankets on your skin, the fact that you can enjoy coffee with cream and sugar – everything is a blessing! Thank God for your small blessings and he will bless you even more. God is always listening. Life is meant to be enjoyed and every day we wake up is another opportunity to enjoy it.

It is so much easier to see how I had lost my voice and the process of regaining it, and the strength that was born within me. My life has been difficult, but by lifting the veil and seeing the small blessings, it has made all the difference. One might ask, that with such trauma, how can I even breathe unrestricted? I have learned to look for the joys in small things. Just getting up in the morning and sitting on my small patio with a cup of coffee and the birds singing in the trees as the sun rises. That is enough although a hot bubble bath at least five days a week is like topping this bliss with whipped cream. The words "thank you God" automatically come out of my mouth as my muscles relax.

This is an affirmation I began to say every morning and at night before I fall asleep or sometimes when I remember during the day, and I want to share it with you. EVERYDAY AND IN EVERYWAY, I AM GETTING BETTER AND BETTER – IN JESUS' NAME... *EVERYDAY AND IN EVERYWAY, I AM GETTING BETTER AND BETTER – IN JESUS' NAME.*

I realize not everyone is christian, and I am inviting you to insert the name that holds true to your beliefs. Personally, I've let go of a lot of the religious traditions in my life, but I've never let go of God. I've had some very dark lonely times in my life, but I've always kept my connection with Jesus. I don't have a lot but I have Jesus!!

I am so grateful for the small things and all the great things in my life! I get to have conversations with my children, travel and make great memories with them. I am blessed to work with wonderful men and women that serve our community. Sometimes life happens and the weight on our shoulders feels so heavy and endless. We feel defeated. Turn it over to God. He knows your heart, and he knows your burden. Talk to Him and listen for his response. Even when it's bad it's good.

ACKNOWLEDGEMENTS

Writing a book was a rollercoaster of emotions and harder than I expected. This work would not have been completed and published without the support of Alicia Dunams, Book Strategist, and CEO of Bestseller in a Weekend (bestsellerinaweekend. com), and her team. I would especially like to thank my ever-patient Editor, Susan Nunn for her guidance and empathy. Every one of our conversations was like a healing therapy session for me. Thank you, you are amazing Susan! To all the friends that kept tabs on me through this process: thank you guys for checking in, your support meant a lot to me.

Nobody has been more important to me in the pursuit of this project than my children. My Sarayi, you are the unending inspiration in my life - thank you momma.

To book Sara Paredes as a speaker for your next event, or for your podcast, email her at sarmarpar@yahoo.com or follow her on Instragram at @Makeupartistsarita.

GLOSSARY

Ave Maria -   Hail Mary (used as an expression when in shock).

Ay-   Oh.

Ba or Va-   Go or going to do.

Cahuama-   Slang for 32oz. beer.

Caldo-   Broth or soup/stew.

Chapulin-   Grasshopper.

Chayo/Chayito-   Nick name/term of endearment/AKA for a person named Rosario.

Chepa/Chepita-   Nick name/term of endearment/AKA for a person named Josefa.

Colorado-   Red.

Comadre-   Your child's Godparent is your Comadre (feminine) /Compadre (masculine).

Coyotas-   Traditional cookies from Hermosillo, Sonora made from flour and brown sugar.

Cuates-   Slang for twins.

De-   Of/ being from.

Dios-	God.
Dona -	Ma'am/Mrs.
Esos-	Those
Guaymas-	City in the state of Sonora, located in northern Mexico.
Huera/ro-	Nick name/term of endearment/AKA for a person with light hair and fair skin.
Juchitlan-	A town in the state of Jalisco, central Mexico.
La-	The used when referring to a female.
Lavar-	Wash.
Llave-	Spanner/wrench/key
Los-	The used when referring to multiple males or male and female.
Mija/jo-	Darling/sweetie/ term of endearment used for a female.
Nacio-	Born
Nana-	How most people in Northern Mexico refer to their grandmother.
Nevenario-	Novena. A recitation of a prayer for nine consecutive days.
Oye-	Hey/Look here.
Pancho-	Nick name/term of endearment/AKA for a person named Francisco.
Pasame-	Pass me.
Pendeja-	Use when referring to a very stupid person.
Platos-	Dishes.
Puricima-	Purest/immaculate used when referring to Mary, Mother of God.

Quien-	Who.
Reina-	Queen.
Saladitos-	Salted Plums.
Sarita-	Nick name/term of endearment/AKA for a person named Sara.
Tata-	How most people in Northern Mexico refer to their grandfather.
Tia-	Aunt.
Tio-	Uncle.
Tuercas-	Screw.
Y-	And.
Yo-	Me.

www.ingramcontent.com/pod-product-compliance
Lightning Source LLC
Chambersburg PA
CBHW021236090426
42740CB00006B/566